CW00663018

ON THE YACHTS

Published in Scotland by JRM Publishing
07967 227 016
jrmacgregor@aol.com

Copyright © 2019 James MacGregor & Robbie MacKenzie

The rights of James MacGregor and Robbie MacKenzie to
be identified as authors of this work have been asserted in
accordance with the Copyright, Designs and Patents Act 1988.

All rights reserved. No part of this book may be reprinted or reproduced or utilized
in any form or by any electronic, mechanical, or other means, now known or
hereafter invented, including photocopying and recording, or in any information
storage or retrieval system, without permission in writing from the publishers.

British Library Cataloguing in Publication Data
A catalogue record for this book is available from the British Library

ISBN 978-1-9160390-0-1

Image of *Roska* General Arrangement Drawing used on
front and back cover is supplied courtesy of Mylne Yacht Design

Cover design and typesetting – Kerrie Moncur Design & Typesetting
kmdesigntypesetting@hotmail.com

Print managed by Jellyfish Solutions Ltd.

ON THE
YACHTS

LOCHBROOM SEAMEN 1880-1950

JAMES MACGREGOR
ROBBIE MACKENZIE

WILLIAM MACGREGOR
1.8.1912 - 23.3.1973

MURDO ALLAN MACKENZIE
6.8.1952 - 26.2.2012

CONTENTS

ACKNOWLEDGEMENTS

We wish to thank Ullapool Museum for permission to reproduce many photographs from their collection as part of this publication.

The origins of this book lie in the 2014 Ullapool Museum exhibition *A Community at Sea*, and the different strands of research which preceded it. That exhibition and this book could not have been produced without the past photographic contributions of the various Lochbroom families to the Ullapool Museum, and their specific assistance to this project. Mention is also due to Pauline Ward, Veronica Vossen Wood and Helen Avenell who assisted Robbie with producing *A Community at Sea*.

It is now difficult to separately identify the sources of all the images originally provided by these families, and regrettably many are simply credited to the Ullapool Museum. We sincerely hope that the families concerned will recognise their past donations. We gratefully acknowledge these contributions, and wish to apologise to those whose relatives may have been overlooked or otherwise referenced incorrectly in this publication. Unfortunately, we are now a generation too late to make a perfect record of this part of Lochbroom's history.

The now deceased Duncan "Tor" MacKenzie and Alec "Lally" MacKenzie provided most of the yachting related images to the Museum. They were also very important in terms of supplying the Museum with descriptions of the people depicted, and other information. We regret they did not live to see their material used in this way.

In addition to the "older" photographs, the following persons (listed alphabetically) provided information and "new" photographs to assist the current publication; Alex Eaton, Tessa Evans, Christine Harvey, Tania Hutchison, Mary MacCrimmon, Angie MacKenzie (Allan), Duncan MacKenzie (Bain), Eric MacKenzie, Finlay MacKenzie (Buie), MacNab MacKenzie (Nabby), Maymie MacKenzie (Tanera), Sandy MacKenzie, Willie MacKenzie (Jock), Ian MacLean, John MacLeod (Raigie), Mary MacLeod (Cloudy), Audrey Megbeghandu (Skene), Donald Miller, Kenny Munro, Peter Newling, Jessie Osborne, Kate Rettie, Diyanne Ross, Ann Urquhart, Gordon Urquhart.

Every effort has been made to trace all copyright holders, and where possible these are acknowledged in the text and listed below. We apologise if photographs have been used without due credit, and for related errors or omissions.

For images of the yachts not available locally, we gratefully acknowledge the generous assistance of the following;

- William Collier of GL Watson for historical images marked GL WATSON
- Ben Wood of Island Images for use of his beautiful modern photographs of *Mariquita,* and for assistance with use of Guido Cantini images
- Iain McAllister of Sandeman Yacht Company for photograph of *Mariquita* crew cabin
- Marc Turner of PFM Pictures for the GLA Blair photograph of *Vadura* on the Clyde
- Nottage Maritime Institute, Essex for permission (August 2018) to use the image of the *Vanessa/Golden Eagle* on the Colne
- Jon Johnson of Portree for recent photograph of *Kentra*

The following are thanked for assistance in obtaining modern images of *Roska* and *Jeano*;

- Miguel Lamas Pardo for facilitating contacts in Spain regarding the *Arosa (ex Roska)*
- Salvador Omil Pereira of the Escuela Naval Militar (Spanish Navy) for permission (3rd May 2018) to use modern images of the *Arosa* (ex *Roska*)
- Shipoak Saikat for facilitating contacts in Brazil regarding the *Cisne Branco* (ex *Jeano*)
- Sergio Esteves of Abravela Sail Training Academy, Brazil for 1980s image of *Jeano* (as *Cisne Branco*) in 1980 (25th May 2018)

Licenses to reproduce images of certain boats have been obtained from the following;

- Kenneth Beken (May 2018 and May 2019) for the images marked PHOTO © BEKEN
- Picture Library at Scott Polar Research Institute, University of Cambridge (August 2018) for the image of the *Gleniffer* at Lamlash
- Scottish Fisheries Museum, Anstruther (1st June 2018) for the image of the Zulu lugger
- Historic Environment Scotland for photo of William MacGregor with the Land Court in 1948, and the 1920s Crossley mail bus in Ullapool
- Alamy stock images for the modern photographs of *Thendara, Mariella* and *Belle Aventure* (ex. *Eileen*), and old images of *Astra, Oriana* and *Anna Marie*

Thanks are also due for other graphics, as follows;

- Christine Harvey for photos and the reference letter provided by Andrew MacGeorge to her father John MacLean in September 1939
- Ian and Murdo MacLean for MacLean reference letters
- Finlay MacKenzie for reference letter written by Danie "Buie" MacKenzie
- Sandy MacKenzie for John MacKenzie's reference letters from William Wordie and others
- Ullapool Museum for extracts from Kenneth MacRae seaman's discharge book

- The Willie MacKenzie painting of *Gleniffer* was loaned to the Ullapool Museum by Jessie Osborne, and the photograph was supplied by William Collier of GL Watson
- Ann Urquhart for image of the *Yachting Cook Book* used by Danny Urquhart
- Bill Bishop (www.bishopmarineart.com) for permission (22nd April 2018) to reproduce his painting *"15-Metres off Cowes before 1914"*
- The image of Andrew MacGeorge's Rolls Royce is reproduced courtesy of Ian Johnstone of The Real Car Co. Ltd (30th May 2018)
- David Gray at Mylne Yacht Design for permission (16th April 2018) to use the General Arrangement drawing of the *Roska*
- Donald Fullerton of Helensburgh Heritage Trust for permission (19th May 2018) to reproduce images of the *Ardenvohr* and *Kilmahew* houses
- Old pictures of Loch Broom Lochside, Wylie & Lochhead store and Paisleys Outfitters, Glasgow are from postcards originally published by JB White and J McCulloch (Caledonia Series)
- Alamy stock images for the Allan Line advertising poster

The following images are available online with no known restrictions;
- America's Cup related photographs of 1893-1903 from the US Library of Congress
- *James Craig* – restored square-rigged ship in Sydney Harbour
- *Dunselma,* Fowler Memorial Clock, Anchor Mills, Lochside hills and others from the *geograph* site
- Engraving of steam yacht *Norseman* at opening of Manchester Ship Canal

Keith Whittles of Whittles Publishing, Dunbeath advised and assisted with printing and publishing, and Kerrie Moncur, Thurso, designed the cover, typeset and prepared the book for printing.

Finally, the Yachting Historical Society has produced a digital version of past editions of Lloyds Register of Yachts, which was most useful in tracing the ownership history of the old yachts.

We sincerely hope we have not omitted to mention any individual or organisation that assisted.

INTRODUCTION

This book contains a collection of photographs taken in the early part of the 20th century onboard some of the finest sailing and steam yachts of the era. Working men from Wester Ross are pictured on famous boats such as *Thendara, Vadura* and *Lulworth*, some of which have been expensively restored in the modern era. The men in the photographs are from the coastal communities around Ullapool, mainly from upper Loch Broom ("the Lochside") but also further afield.

The photographs originated in several different private collections, but many have found their way into the archive organised by the Ullapool Museum. This resource has made it possible to produce a permanent record of the relatively unknown involvement of this remote North West Highland community in the leisure pursuits of the wealthiest people of those times.

Long before yachting became a pastime within reach of the ordinary person, it was an activity restricted to the very rich. Large and costly yachts were built for cruising and racing and as a means of demonstrating one's wealth and social status. In the UK, the heyday of this type of yachting extended from the 1870s to the 1930s. Many of the boats from that era, their designers, and the races in which they competed, were famous in their own time and are still celebrated today. The Loch Broom men worked on yachts from the drawing boards of Watson, Fife and Mylne, and on boats owned by tycoons such as Lipton, Coats, Clark and Singer. The list of names reads like a "Who's Who" of the industrial and yachting world from the Victorian Age to World War Two.

Unlike today, the gentlemen owners of that era did not generally sail their own yachts but employed professional seamen to do so. Loch Broom men had worked at sea for generations, often as self-employed fishermen in their home waters, or as hired crew on the big East Coast herring luggers. Like other fishermen, they were well equipped with the skills and physical strength needed to crew the sailing yachts of some of Britain's wealthiest families.

In the years prior to the outbreak of World War Two, crewing on such yachts provided a welcome form of income for the seamen of Loch Broom district and other parts of the West Highlands and Islands. This form of employment offered a guaranteed cash income, in stark contrast to the uncertain returns from fishing and subsistence agriculture. Particularly in the years before World War One, the money earned by these men made an important contribution to the economy of the Ullapool area.

In addition, the seasonal nature of the work allowed the seamen to earn money without having to emigrate or spend virtually all their time away from home on deep sea merchant vessels. As a result, the descendants of many of the men illustrated in these photographs can still be found in the Ullapool area, and are known by the same bynames as their ancestors.

As well as presenting the yachting photographs from various Ullapool archives, this book aims to provide biographical details for some of the men of Loch Broom who were employed on these famous yachts, documenting their lives along with the details of the vessels and their owners.

WORKING ON THE YACHTS

Historical Context

King Charles II was introduced to *jachts* during his temporary 17th century exile in the Netherlands and brought this sport back to England on his return in 1660. At that time yachting was limited to a very select few and it was not until the 1800s that yachting grew rapidly in popularity in England. Following the end of the Napoleonic wars, coastal waters became safe for pleasure craft as well as working vessels. At the same time, the rising prosperity of the middle and upper classes, fuelled by the Industrial Revolution, led to a rapid expansion in leisure pastimes, which included yacht cruising and racing.

Gradually, the owners of the larger yachts organised themselves into yacht clubs and established races over prescribed courses under specified rules. Bigger and faster yachts were built to win these races, and this led to a technological competition, continued into recent times by the contest for the America's Cup. This particular event dates from 1851, when *America*, a visiting schooner from the USA, defeated the local English yachts in a race around the Isle of Wight.

The prestige associated with the largest and most costly of these yachts attracted royalty and captains of industry into ownership. In the UK, most of the yacht racing took place in the Solent and on the Clyde, but a sequence of regattas was organised at other places around the coast over the summer months.

These races began to achieve greater prominence with the arrival of photography in the later part of the 19th century, and big crowds were attracted to follow the sport. The large size of the boats helped spectators at suitable viewing points to see the action taking place on courses laid out to pass close inshore.

In 1885, despite bad weather, interest in racing was such that two packed Clyde excursion steamers followed a pair of yachts owned by the Clark and Coats thread-making families from Paisley on a 60-mile race around Ailsa Craig. In the West Country in July 1894, people came by train from all over southwest England to watch the Mount's Bay Regatta in which the America's Cup winner *Vigilant* owned by Jay Gould, director of the American Cable Company, took on the Prince of Wales's *Britannia*. The skippers were working men; two Nicholls brothers who were ship pilots from Penzance. Earlier the same year, *Vigilant*, *Britannia* and the British America's Cup challenger *Valkyrie II* raced on the Clyde watched by 100,000 spectators.

In the Clyde area, yachting regattas were covered by no fewer than nine specialist newspaper correspondents and several specialist photographers. Some of this public interest can be explained by the limited alternative spectator sports during the summer months, and the presence of large numbers of working people spending their annual summer vacation "*doon the watter*" in the coastal resorts.

Until 1914, there was steady growth in yacht cruising and racing in the UK, although the interest in yachting slowed somewhat towards the end of the 1890s, especially for "big class" racing. This dip occurred for several reasons, including the introduction of death duties in 1894, depressed agricultural prices, and the death of Queen Victoria in 1901. Also, the motor car was becoming the latest craze among the rich.

From about 1906 there was a resurgence of interest when different classes of yachts of "standardised" design appeared, such as the 15-Metre and 19-Metre International Rule boats. This renewed enthusiasm was terminated by the declaration of war on 4th August 1914 (the eve of Cowes Week), and the cruising scene also came to an abrupt end. Ullapool's James Matheson [19] recorded that, "*.....those who remember the days leading up to the declaration of war speak of a crowded village – hotels and guest houses full. The shooting lodge guests were all up for the Glorious Twelfth, and the bay was full of yachts. By the afternoon all these people just disappeared*".

Many owners and paid hands belonged to the Royal Naval Reserve and were called up, and others also immediately volunteered for service. As well as the personal risk involved, for the paid racing hands and their families this also represented a financial sacrifice as they were just about to enter the most lucrative part of the season.

There was no racing in the UK from 1914 to 1918 and many British yachts were sold to neutral Scandinavia at that time. Larger steam and motor yachts were requisitioned for auxiliary naval duties. One of these was the *Amalthaea* (ex *Iolanthe*), renamed as *HMY Iolaire* and forever associated with the tragedy on 1st January 1919 when she was lost outside Stornoway harbour, carrying Lewis and Harris sailors returning from World War One.

The conflict at sea and on land provided less pleasant forms of employment for the men from Loch Broom and elsewhere. Many yacht owners and crew lost their lives or were permanently disabled in body or mind. For the survivors of all classes, the war changed many aspects of the economy and way of life. As well as a general loss of optimism, there was a great inflation in the cost of many things including labour, so that the rich were less able to employ large numbers of personnel in their homes and on their yachts.

However, in 1919 King George V decided to have the royal racing yacht *Britannia* fitted out for the 1920 season, and this stimulated other owners to begin racing again. As a result, big yacht racing survived through the inter-war period.

The period between 1924 and 1930 is famous for the so-called Big Five, consisting of *Britannia* along with *Lulworth, White Heather II, Shamrock,* and the schooner *Westward.* They were joined at the regattas by the modern Bermudan rigged yachts, *Astra, Cambria* and *Candida* from 1928, and the America's Cup challenger *Shamrock V* in 1930. This was the year which saw the introduction of the famous J class yachts, and what some see as the golden age of this kind of yachting.

Once again, this era was short-lived, as UK yachting activity was depressed in 1936 by the death of King George V, marked by the scuttling of his *Britannia* off the Isle of Wight. In 1937, the last America's Cup contest for 21 years took place, and this can be seen as the beginning of the end of Big Yacht racing. The outbreak of World War Two in September 1939 sealed the fate of this style of yachting.

Furthermore, even by 1935, inshore course racing with large, specialised yachts was becoming too expensive for many, and people were turning their attention to offshore racing in smaller boats. The Fastnet Race and other ocean races of today stem from this inter-war period. At the same time, the 1920s and 1930s saw several classic cruising yachts built on the Clyde for local owners to designs by Alfred Mylne, including *Vadura, Roska* and *Thendara.*

Many of the Clyde and other yachts were requisitioned in 1939 and 1940 by the British government. They were used as patrol vessels and for deploying barrage balloon screens to protect the convoys that assembled in the Firth of Clyde and elsewhere from attack by German bombers. The premises of many sailing clubs were also requisitioned as they provided exactly the locations and facilities considered useful by the military. Several large yachts were scrapped for their lead and steel content as part of the war effort.

Some limited racing and cruising with the surviving pre-war boats resumed after 1945, but the employment opportunities for professional yachtsmen in UK waters were greatly reduced. Nowadays, a new class of internationally mobile professional crew tends to the yachts of the extremely rich in locations such as the Cote d'Azur and Antigua. Some of the yachts on which they work are survivors from the era described in this book, often restored at great expense.

The Clyde as a Yachting Centre

In the UK the Clyde rapidly became a centre for yachting second only to Cowes, with several different clubs active. The Scott's shipyard at Greenock is believed to have built the first yacht in Scotland in 1803. By 1902 the Royal Clyde Yacht Club alone had 1000 members and over 400 yachts. Two Clyde yacht clubs challenged for the America's Cup - the Royal Northern in 1886 and the Royal Clyde one year later.

Many famous yachts were produced on the Clyde by designers and builders such as GL Watson, the Fifes and Alfred Mylne, and later McGruer & Co and David Boyd. The Royal Yacht *Britannia*

America's Cup race 1903 – RELIANCE & SHAMROCK III
(US Library of Congress)

could be seen racing there along with many other famous big yachts. During the 1920s and 1930s the Clyde yacht clubs competed successfully with American yacht clubs in both team racing and match racing.

The Clyde area produced several famous racing yacht skippers, including Archie Hogarth of Bute, and the Barr brothers from Gourock (Charlie Barr won the America's Cup three times, sailing for the USA). Both the Barrs and Hogarths were fishing families.

The Yachting Season

John Leather has written extensively of the lives of the Essex coast seamen of the late 19th and early 20th century, several of whom became famous yachting skippers, including Edward Sycamore, Lemon Cranfield and his brothers [9,14]. The experiences of these men from the Colne and Blackwater rivers would have been similar in some ways to that of the West Highland men on the Clyde yachts, and this book draws on his writings.

After the spring fitting out period, the British yacht racing season began at Harwich in Essex at the beginning of May, and the yachts then sailed clockwise around the coast, taking part in

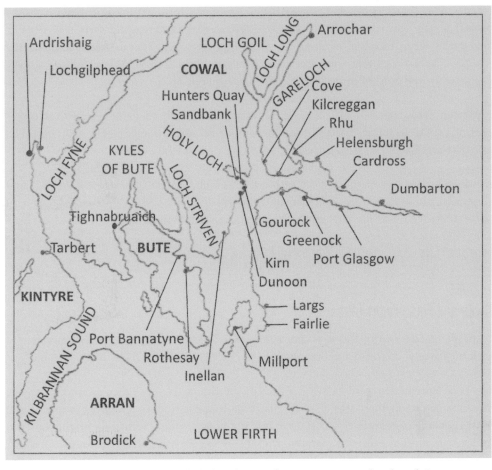

Above: Map of the Firth of Clyde – showing locations associated with yachting

Below: Yachts Racing on the Clyde, late 1930s – taken from ROSKA
(MacGregor photo)

regattas at Southend, Dover and Bangor, before spending a fortnight racing on the Clyde. The boats then returned to the south coast for Cowes Week and the Ryde Regatta. The Cowes Regatta, held during the first week of August, was one of the great occasions of the social calendar. The season ended in September, with a regatta at Dartmouth and Torbay. Visits to Europe (usually Kiel) and the east coast of Ireland were sometimes required.

Navigation of the racing yacht between these regattas was usually left to the crew with no owner present. For safe handling, smaller trysails were used instead of the huge racing mainsails which were too large for serious passage-making work.

At the end of the season, most of the yachts were laid up for the winter. Their West Highland crews returned to the family croft or found employment on merchant ships and fishing boats. Some worked in Clydeside shipbuilding and repair yards until the following spring.

Yacht Clubs

Clyde and Forth Yacht Clubs

In the photographs within this book, the men are usually pictured wearing a jersey embroidered with the name of the yacht and the initials of the yacht club to which the owner belonged.

The Loch Broom men were mainly connected with the yacht clubs based around the Clyde. This was natural as there was a strong maritime connection between Glasgow and all the West Highland communities at that time. In a region where roads were poor or non-existent, and people did not own cars, communications by MacBrayne's steamers were convenient for most people. As already described, the Clyde had become a leading yachting centre, and there were many successful businessmen in the area with the wherewithal to engage in the sport.

Consequently, the acronyms RCYC (Royal Clyde Yacht Club) and RNYC (Royal Northern Yacht Club) are seen most frequently on the jerseys of the Loch Broom men in these photographs.

Some men sport jerseys from the RFYC (Royal Forth Yacht Club). Although less famous than its counterparts to the west, this club can trace its formation back to 1868, and even earlier origins. It incorporates the Royal Eastern Yacht Club (founded in 1835) and the Almond Yacht Club (founded in 1897).

Royal Clyde Yacht Club (RCYC) and Royal Northern Yacht Club (RNYC)

These two clubs dominated the Scottish yachting scene from the late 19th to the early 20th century, with programmes of grand regattas arranged from May to September each year. Both the RNYC and the RCYC grew with the economic development of the Clyde area, with membership including many of the major figures in shipbuilding and thread-making (where the Coats and Clarks of Paisley were prominent).

Many individuals were members of both clubs, and there was considerable co-operation. The two clubs alternated each year in holding the first regatta of the Clyde season. In 1886 the Royal Northern yacht *Galatea* challenged for the America's Cup and the following year it was the turn of *Thistle* from the Royal Clyde [10].

Flags of Yacht Clubs
(Lloyds Register of Yachts, 1937)

The origins of the Royal Northern Yacht Club (RNYC) go back to 1824, when the Scott shipbuilding family of Greenock was prominent in its formation. A Royal Warrant to fly the Blue Ensign was granted in 1831. In 1878, Rothesay became the base for the club's regattas when a wing of the Queen's Hotel (later the Grand Marine Hotel, now converted into apartments) was leased as a clubhouse. The RNYC remained at Rothesay until 1937 when it moved to the 1857 baronial villa *Ardenvohr* at Rhu, near Helensburgh (the present home of the RNCYC), merging with Gareloch Yacht Club at that time.

In 1856, the Clyde Model Yacht Club was formed, proposing to take in only smaller yachts less than 8 tons. It soon dropped the word 'model' from its title and offered racing for much larger yachts. The club instituted the current method of starting yacht races in 1857, with a five minutes interval between the preparatory and the starting signals. It became the Royal Clyde Yacht Club (RCYC) in 1872. In the same year, it established a clubhouse at the Royal Marine Hotel at Hunter's Quay, which it purchased outright a few years later. By 1910, the RCYC was the largest club in the British Isles.

The changing economic climate and reduction in Clyde steamer services made the Hunter's Quay location impractical, and during the early 1950s the RCYC also moved to a smaller base in Rhu.

The Royal Northern & Clyde Yacht Club (RNCYC) of today was formed in 1978 by a merger of these two old Clubs; the Royal Northern and the Royal Clyde.

Clyde Corinthian Yacht Club (CCYC)

This club's initials are not seen so frequently on the jerseys of the Loch Broom men, as the primary objective of the Clyde Corinthian Yacht Club (CCYC) was to avoid the use of professional sailors. Middle-class yacht owners such as lawyers and doctors could not afford the ostentation which characterised aristocratic yachting. Nor did they find it desirable. Instead, they developed their own philosophy; the Corinthian. This term originated in the USA in the mid-nineteenth century to denote a wealthy amateur sportsman, and spread to Britain.

The CCYC was formed in 1876 for amateurs to steer and manage yachts themselves without the aid of professional hands. This amateur status of helmsman and crew was jealously guarded by the members of the CCYC during the professional era. For well over twenty years the founders rejected all efforts for paid hands to be allowed onboard members' yachts while racing. However, yachts became bigger, and by 1898 one paid hand was permitted for certain classes. As well as encouraging racing for amateurs, the club organised races for women as early as 1891.

By 1889 the CCYC accepted an offer from the Royal Clyde Yacht Club for the use of the RCYC clubhouse at Hunter's Quay on the occasion of CCYC races, and in the following year a similar offer from the Royal Northern Yacht Club was accepted for the use of the RNYC clubhouse facilities at Rothesay for Corinthian events.

Ardenvohr – home of
the Royal Northern
Yacht Club (now
RNCYC) from 1937
(Helensburgh
Heritage Trust)

From the time of the CCYC formation, a May regatta was held after the opening event of the Clyde season hosted by the Royal Northern Yacht Club or the Royal Clyde Yacht Club.

What is now the well known Tarbert race originated in 1890 with the CCYC arranging a contest for large cruising yachts to Ardrishaig on a Saturday in early August with a return race on the Monday. In 1894 the finishing point was moved to Tarbert. This race has outlived almost every other event in Clyde yachting, and is sailed under strict amateur rules, until recently without spinnakers.

The Owners

Business Connections on the Clyde

Some of the yachts featured in this book were owned by high profile globe-trotting millionaires such as Kenneth Clark (*Kentra*) and Mortimer Singer (*Lulworth, Astra*), but most of the Loch Broom men worked on boats owned by more down-to-earth personalities from the Glasgow area.

The 19th century industrial development of Clydeside produced individuals with enormous fortunes, well able to afford the construction and upkeep of the finest yachts money could buy. Despite their wealth, many of these owners continued to live locally, and were associated with well-known companies which employed large numbers of ordinary people. Among others, this book features yachts owned by men connected with the firms of Teacher (whisky), Templeton (carpet weaving), Coats and Clark (Paisley thread industry), Fulton (Greenock steel merchants and ship owners) and the Allan Line (ship owning).

In the Glasgow area, many of the yacht owners knew each other professionally and socially as well as at the yacht club. The Clydeside business community had many organisations where these men would meet, and there were also direct family and commercial connections.

Royal Marine Hotel, Hunter's Quay, 1890s, base of RCYC
(US Library of Congress)

At the Royal Troon Golf Club there is a memorial panel to the members who died during World War Two. This lists the Fulton brothers Robert and James (owners of *Eileen*, now *Belle Aventure*) alongside Maurice Clark (owner of *Vadura*).

Another example of these connections is provided by William Wylie who owned *Vida VI* during the 1920s (originally built by Fife of Fairlie in 1906 as *Rose*). He was an owner of the outfitting and furniture firm of Wylie & Lochhead which sometimes contracted to provide the interiors for yachts built at Fairlie. He lived on the same Glasgow street as Andrew MacGeorge of *Roska*.

The Stephen shipbuilding yard at Linthouse in Glasgow produced several of the yachts featured in this book, and the yard owners were at the centre of many of these yachting relationships. Several generations of the Stephen family were keen sailors who knew their yacht ordering clients personally, and indeed were sometimes related to them. In Victorian times, Alex Stephen and James Templeton of the carpet manufacturing firm had married each other's sisters. Later, Arthur Young (owner of *Thendara,* built at Linthouse in 1937) was born in 1899 to a daughter of the Templeton family [8,12]. The Stephens and Arthur Young attended the 1932 funeral of family friend Robert S Allan (owner of the steam yacht *Sheila*). Stephens had built many ships for the Allan Line.

Fred J Stephen (1863-1932) ran the shipyard from 1916 to 1932 and found the time to design his own 3-ton yacht *Coila* in 1886, followed by *Coila II* in 1908. He also had the 6-Metre *Coila III* and the 8-Metre *Coila IV* (1924). He sailed 670 races in these boats, winning about 440 prizes, 256 of them firsts [7].

In 1922, his son John Graeme Stephen (1894-1970) won the Seawanhaka Cup in the USA helming his father's 6-Metre *Coila III*. John Stephen was also a crew member in Arthur Young's 8-Metre *Saskia* which successfully saw off the American Seawanhaka Club challengers in Scottish waters in 1931. John became Shipyard Director on his father's death in 1932, and his older brother Murray took over as Chairman and Managing Director.

Arthur Young and Maurice Clark ordered their Mylne designed cruising yachts (*Thendara, Vadura*) from Stephen. During the 1930s they were colleagues in British teams challenging the USA in the 6-Metre and other classes. The designer Mylne would, of course, have been well known to both owners and builder. Mylne was himself a first-class helmsman and won many races.

In 1937, Arthur Young (*Thendara*) and Andrew MacGeorge (*Roska*) were senior officers of the Loch Long Sailing Club. Along with J H Maurice Clark (*Vadura*), they were also officers of the Mudhook Club. These people also served together as officers of other clubs.

Costs for the Owner

Apart from the capital cost of purchasing the yacht (details are given in a later chapter), the owners of these vessels required sufficient funds to pay the wages of the crew and many other expenses.

According to John Leather, for the owner of a 15-Metre class racing yacht in the period around 1910, the crew would cost approximately as follows [9,14];

- Skipper - £150
- Mate - 22 weeks at 32 shillings (£35 4s)
- Cook and steward – 22 weeks at 32 shillings each per week (£35 4s)
- 5 Hands – 22 weeks at 26 shillings (about £1.30) each per week (£143), plus any special allowances for bowsprit end and masthead men
- "Grub money" allowance of 2 shillings and sixpence for each racing day - 50 starts (£50)
- Prize money or starting money extra

Other expenses for this size of yacht would have included;

- Racing pilot if required - 30 shillings each race where used
- Entrance fees and other expenses - £100
- Clothes for Skipper and crew - £69
- Hauling out the yacht and scrubbing for racing - £60
- Insurance - £35
- Laying up yacht for winter and sundry items - £100

The crew costs would vary with the yacht size, with a 19-Metre and 23-Metre requiring a total complement of about 14 and 24, respectively, compared to nine on a 15-Metre. The difference was in the size of the deck squad, where the 20 men on a 23-Metre cost twice as much as the ten on a 19-Metre, and four times as much as the five on a 15-Metre.

In return for the above outlay, a 15-Metre yacht might hope to win about £250 prize money during an average season, although the top yachts and their skippers could win much greater sums. The monetary prizes offered for the 19-Metre Class before World War One varied, but £30-40 first prize and £15-20 second prize were typical amounts, the first sometimes replaced or supplemented by a silver cup or other trophy. Cash prizes could only slightly offset an owner's expenses for the season.

In 1911 the total cost of owning a 19-Metre during a season from mid-April to mid-September was in the region of £1,800 or £2,000. Despite the economy compared to the £5,000 annual running costs of a 23-Metre, only wealthy men could afford to own a racer of this size. For the smaller 15-Metre yachts the cost might be around £1,500.

In contrast, the average earnings of the Scottish herring fleet at the 1911 autumn (East Anglia) fishing were only £193 for each of the sailing boats, and £665 for the steam drifters. For the summer fishing the corresponding sums were £281 and £887, respectively [11]. These sums had to be divided over the crew after expenses were deducted.

The Paid Hands

Crew Sizes

The crew numbers varied with the size of the yacht and her owner's preference to engage in serious racing or cruising. For example, in 1922 a 120ft cruising schooner would employ a crew of 15, including Skipper, Mate, second mate, six hands, engineer, three stewards and two cooks.

Early gaff rigged racing cutters had 30-35 men to provide hauling power as these yachts had few if any winches – all rope hauling was originally done with human muscle and blocks and tackles.

In contrast, the large gaff cutter *Lulworth* of the 1920s used a smaller racing crew of 26, and this was considered too few, owing to the heaviness of her gear. In 1933 the big modern racing cutter *Astra* had a crew of 18. The simpler Bermudan rig of this design meant that there was no mainsail gaff to hoist, nor any gaff topsail to handle.

The effect of vessel size is shown in the typical crew sizes for different International Rule racing craft. The larger boats did not have more sails, but the manpower needed to haul and handle the gear went up roughly in proportion to the sail area. As mentioned above, a 15-Metre racing yacht with 4,500 ft² sail would have a total crew size of about nine, including five deckhands.

RELIANCE crew hoisting the Mainsail - 1903 America's Cup
(US Library of Congress)

This would rise to 14 with ten hands on a 19-Metre with 6,200 ft², and 24 with 20 hands on a 23-Metre with 10,000 ft².

Depending on the force of the wind, on a big racer without winches it could take up to 40 men to hoist the 2 tonnes of mainsail and gaff, and then 20 hands to sheet in the sail using the 4-inch diameter mainsheet.

Selection

The owners of the yachts employed experienced seafarers from the coastal communities to man and skipper their yachts. At the turn of the last century most fishing vessels were still engineless, and so there was a ready pool of men for whom harnessing the power of the wind and tides was second nature. In the UK, the Colne and Blackwater creeks in Essex, Blakeney in Norfolk, Brixham in Devon, the Solent and the Firth of Clyde villages were favourite sources of crew.

Many racing yacht owners were as ruthlessly competitive in their sailing as in their business dealings. Having bought or commissioned the best available yachts, they were also willing to pay good wages for the best skipper and crew, plus a share of any prize money. Crews were rigged out at the owner's expense, with shoes, oilskins, trousers and jerseys embroidered with the name of their yacht.

On the racing boats, the skippers had to be experts in tactics, gauging the weather, and extracting the best performance from the crew and boat. Away from the race course, care and skill were required when getting the engineless vessel in and out of harbour. The skipper's practical experience came from years of sailing different types of small craft, usually fishing boats, often continuing during the winter months when the yachts were laid up. Considerable confidence was required to move from such humble craft and take responsibility for large and costly yachts under the eyes of their powerful owners.

It is not known how the first men from the North West Highlands found employment of this sort. Several of the Clyde yacht owners were also shipping magnates and may have been able to select their yacht crew via their normal seafarer recruitment channels. West Highland and Hebridean seamen were well represented in the crews of the deep sea merchant fleet at that time and for many years after, and would have been in a good position to become aware of and take up such opportunities. It is also possible that the involvement began through connections with friends or relatives on the Clyde who had previously found work on the yachts. Whatever the method of initiation, one Lochside man probably had the good fortune to secure the first position, and word of mouth led to more and more of his friends and relations becoming involved.

Other districts of the West Coast also had a strong involvement in yachting, including Tighnabruaich on the Kyles of Bute, Tarskavaig on Skye, parts of Harris and Gairloch. In the Gairloch area there were three yacht skippers from Port Henderson, including John Watson who captained the yacht of the Wills family (cigarette manufacturers) for 30 years.

The Skipper would normally have responsibility for recruiting the rest of the crew. Originally a Skipper was likely to choose only men from his own district, but by the 1930s the crews of the top racing boats tended to be mixed, with men selected on merit rather than origin or personal relationships. However, from the photographs of the Loch Broom men, it seems clear that they found employment as teams, even into the 1930s.

Many amateurs were considered useful hands, but they were not as fast as the professional crews when racing, and not able to pull the same weight on a rope. Most amateurs were not used to manual work, and their soft hands suffered terribly. As one paid hand said, *"You could always tell an amateur from a professional; the galvanised wire and the sheets (ropes) took the skin off the amateur's hands, but the professional's hands took the galvanising off the wire".*

Living Arrangements

In a large yacht, the crew lived in the fo'c'sle with tiers of pipe cots on each side. Lockers on each side served as seats. There would sometimes be a separate cabin for the Skipper. On a 19-Metre racing boat (62 feet waterline length, 17 feet beam), a typical arrangement would be as follows, reading from forward to aft;

- Forecastle for crew, with seat lockers and folding canvas sleeping cots above
- Small cabin for Skipper and a galley arranged to port and starboard in way of the mast
- Saloon for owners amidships
- Two single berth cabins, owner's cabin and toilet aft

The General Arrangement drawing of the slightly smaller ketch *Roska* (waterline length 51 feet, beam 15.75 feet) is reproduced elsewhere in this book and shows the interior layout of a reasonably large cruising yacht. Again, reading from forward to aft, this boat was laid out as follows;

- Forecastle for crew, with seat lockers and 6 folding canvas sleeping cots above (2 port, 4 starboard), with a crew toilet located right forward
- Mast and engine located on centreline towards aft end of the crew's living space – galley located aft and to port side inside this space
- Saloon amidships
- Owner's toilet with bath - to starboard side aft of saloon
- Two single berth cabins each with basin - located to port and starboard
- Third cabin with two single berths, basin and the mizzen mast - located aft, with access from saloon

By the standards of today, onboard facilities were rather basic, even for the owners, but these living arrangements would not have presented any problem for the West Highland men, used to modest conditions at home and at sea. When the involvement with yachting started, many of them would have been living in thatched "black houses". Electricity only came to the Lochside after World War Two.

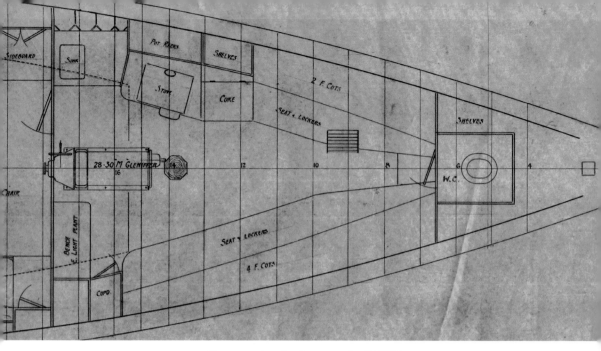

Crew quarters for 6 men on the ROSKA
(Mylne Yacht Design)

Crew quarters with folding cots in 19-Metre yacht MARIQUITA
(Sandeman Yacht Company)

Fitting Out and Laying Up

Before the start of the cruising or racing season, crews would join the yachts at the owner's home port or some well-known yacht lay-up centre. On the Clyde, small harbours on the north side of the Firth such as Hunter's Quay and Innellan were used for this purpose. Some yachts started their season fitting out in specialist yards – like the famous Camper & Nicholson at Gosport on the South Coast of England.

During this period, the yacht would be rigged and made ready for the season, and this demanded skilled boat maintenance, painting, varnishing, and repair work, in addition to the seamanship skills which would be required later in the season.

At the end of the season, the process would be reversed and the yacht laid up for the winter. The sails and running rigging would be taken ashore for storage, possibly with the spars and standing rigging also. A preservative coating might be applied over the varnish and bright metal work, and sometimes the decks. An awning would be rigged to keep the rain and snow off the boat.

The standard of workmanship learned on these high-quality yachts was not forgotten when back at home, and many of the former Loch Broom yachtsmen demonstrated very high standards of skill throughout their lives in all the tasks associated with boat care and maintenance.

Far left: Deck scrubbing team on steam yacht ARIANA - Hugh MacKenzie (left) & Roderick "Crubag" MacKenzie (Kate Rettie photo)

Left: Lally (Alec MacKenzie) varnishing or otherwise maintaining an unidentified mast (Ullapool Museum)

Normal Crew Duties

The hired skipper was responsible for navigating the boat between various racing venues, and also for racing the yacht at regattas if required by the owner.

Even into the 1920s many owners did not take any part in the navigation or handling of the yachts – usually just taking an occasional spell at the wheel in fine weather under the watchful eye of the Skipper or Mate. However, some owners such as Arthur Young (*Thendara*) and Maurice Clark (*Vadura*) were expert helmsmen, with skills honed on the smaller 6-Metre and 8-Metre race boats.

Crew duties on passage included the usual sail handling, hauling on sheets and halyards, tending gear and watch keeping, while in harbour there would be the routine scrubbing down and general maintenance work.

Duties during Racing

At the start of each season the Mate would assign the duties for each man during racing. For example, one man would be allocated the specific task of making fast and letting go the halyards of the mainsail and the spinnaker, while others would be nominated as mastheadsmen with duties including spotting for wind and breaking the topsail out of its stops.

Aboard a big racer on competition days, the working day would start around 6 am with routine tasks such as polishing the brightwork and scrubbing the decks. Sails would be made ready for hoisting and secured in stops (light twine which would break when the sails were pulled into their working positions), before breakfast at 7:30. The mainsail would be set after eating, ready for a start at around 9 am.

Skipper Danie "Buie" MacKenzie watching Owner on tiller
(Ullapool Museum)

Foredeck hands on a fine day
(Ullapool Museum)

Typical positions for the crew would be as follows;
- Skipper at wheel
- Mate and one or two hands in charge of the headsail sheets
- Second mate and two hands in charge of the sheets for the jib topsail, main sheet and topmast sheets
- Mastheadsmen aloft
- Other crew ready on deck to haul on lines where needed
- Usually the cook or steward was in charge of the sails prepared below and ready to send up through the forehatch

The race itself would typically be over a forty to fifty mile course, with the duration dependent on the wind. During racing, the work demanded experienced men able to work quickly and

Foredeck crew on a wet day
(Diyanne Ross photo)

Stowing the sails
(Diyanne Ross photo)

seamlessly together as a team. This was especially necessary on the large boats, which were so powerful that the slightest hesitation or mistake could create a dangerous situation. When not required for sail changes, spare hands were sometimes moved below decks.

After the race, the crew would take the owner and his guests ashore to the yacht club or to his nearby steam yacht. The racer would be anchored and hands would lower the sails and stow them for the next day's racing. Decks would be scrubbed down and minor repairs and maintenance carried out before tea time. After tea, the crew could relax and attempt to dry their clothes around the fo'c'sle stove, before turning in.

In those days Sunday was a day of rest for skippers and crews with no racing. However, on some boats rigging adjustments and some varnishing might be done, depending on the Mate and his attitudes regarding Sunday work and the upkeep of the yacht.

Wages before World War One

Around 1907, a typical basic wage for paid hands on racing yachts was 26 shillings weekly (about £1.30), for a twenty-two week season. Men with special duties received additional allowances. The hands doing duty as mastheadsman and bowspritendsman would each receive from 2 shillings and sixpence to 5 shillings extra per week. The Skipper's wages on a 15-Metre or 19-Metre yacht could be £150 (i.e. £3 per week).

As well as potential prize money, there were additional payments associated with racing, including 5 to 10 shillings "starting money" per race, and "grub money" of 2s 6d for each racing day when food could not be prepared in the normal way. Prize money for a win could be £2 to £5 for the Skipper and £1 per crewman, 16 shillings for second and so on. Prize money was paid at the end of the season by the owner.

For comparison, average wages at John Brown's shipyard on the Clyde in 1914 were £1 16s 8d per week. This had risen to £4 2s per week in 1920. Depending on the fishing, a herring drifter crewman could make £11 in a six or seven-week spell during the season (i.e. £1.6 to £1.8 per week). To put the above in context, in 1900 three dozen eggs could be bought for 1 shilling, one pound (0.45 kg) of butter for 7d, while potatoes were 2 to 3d per stone (6.35 kg). A ship chandler's price list for 1910 shows the following [11];

- Suit of made to measure clothes - £1 12s 6d
- Oilskins - 10s 6d
- Grain hide sea boots – 16s 6d a pair
- Rubber thigh boots – 22s 6d a pair
- Navy blue jersey – 2s 6d to 4s 6d
- Boots – 8s 11d
- Coal – 19s per ton
- Gin – 2s per bottle
- Whisky – 3s 6d per bottle
- Tobacco – 4 ½ d per ounce

RELIANCE crew racing against COLUMBIA in trials for 1903 America's Cup
(US Library of Congress)

At that time, an emigration passage to Canada cost £5 10s third class or £8 10s in a cabin. Around 1910, a West Highland fisherman with access to the necessary funds could get a new 37ft Loch Fyne Skiff sailing fishing vessel built for £100.

The meanings of these pre-decimal currencies are explained in the glossary.

Wages between the Wars

After the war, inflation more than doubled the wages required by the crew. By 1919, an inexperienced Essex yacht hand on an 80ft cruising yacht could earn £3 per week during the summer season, plus 10 shillings per week for good conduct. A racing hand could make £3 17s 6d per week.

Wages onboard *Lulworth* in the 1920s were around £3 a week for seamen, plus another 50p for food and two pints of beer. Being especially at risk, the mastheadman, bobstay men and lee runner man earned an extra 25p danger money. For comparison, unemployment benefit in 1921 was 18s per week, and only for a limited period.

This improved earning power for the working man did not last for long. During the 1920s shipbuilding slump average wages at John Brown's Clyde shipyard fell back from £4 2s per week in 1920 to £2 14s in 1922. During the Great Depression of the 1930s, a labourer's wages were only 40-45s per week.

Foreign going merchant seamen were in a similar position. In the 1930s British able seamen could earn £8 per month, compared to £9 in the 1920s. They also got their food, sometimes of indifferent quantity and quality. Many qualified Master Mariners sailed as ordinary seamen at that time, such was the scarcity of work.

In 1933 yachting wages had also fallen since the early 1920s and Essex racing crews received only £2 14s per week. As before, the mastheadmen and bowsprit men got an extra 5 shillings per week for their potentially dangerous work. Prize money was typically £1 for a win, 15 shillings for a second prize and 5 shillings for a start. Grub money was also paid at a rate of 2s 6d each racing day. West Highland yacht crew wages were similar, with a young hand earning £2 10s for a week's work in 1935.

Food

The Skipper and crew usually paid for and provided their own food. About 1910, the crew would each be pooling 5 shillings (about 20% of their 26s weekly wage) for this purpose. The crew would select one of their number to act as 'caterer' and he used this money to purchase the provisions required by the cook. Hot meals could be prepared on a coal stove in the crew quarters. The crew's cook would generally come to an agreement with the steward who looked after the owner's meals so that leftovers from the saloon table could be used for the crew.

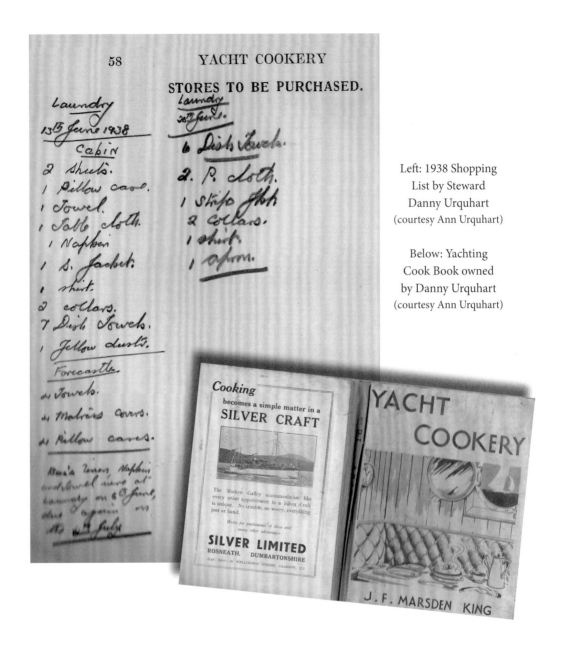

Left: 1938 Shopping List by Steward Danny Urquhart (courtesy Ann Urquhart)

Below: Yachting Cook Book owned by Danny Urquhart (courtesy Ann Urquhart)

The cook, together with the hand who acted as steward, also had to be capable sailors when the yacht was sailing. They usually worked below decks during sail changes, or on deck tending the jib topsail sheets and other foredeck work.

As mentioned previously, all racing hands received a 'grub money' allowance of about 2 shillings and 6 pence for each day of racing when it was impossible to prepare a hot meal.

Clothing and other Perks

In spring, after fitting out was completed, the crew received an allowance of yachting clothes of the best quality paid for by the owner. Paisleys of Jamaica Street, Glasgow were the usual outfitter for the Clyde based yachts. A typical working outfit included;

- Two jerseys with the yacht's name and initials of the yacht club embroidered on the chest
- Two pairs of pilot cloth trousers
- Seaman's cap
- Pair of canvas deck shoes
- Suit of oilskins

Sometimes a dress uniform with double-breasted jacket would be provided, together with a pair of black leather shoes. Another working outfit might also be issued at the start of the fitting out period. Since these clothes would be provided each year, this was a valuable fringe benefit of the job as these items would have been expensive for the men to purchase themselves. Most of the clothes could also be used when back at home. Many of the Loch Broom men in these photographs are wearing yachting jerseys, and they were often worn for many years after the yachting involvement had ceased. Sometimes, if the wearer did not want the logo to be seen, the jersey could be worn back-to-front under a jacket.

Another perk was to take home left-over rope and paint. With their smartly painted houses, the Lochside yachting families were the envy of others, especially Ullapool residents, who did not have the same work opportunity and benefits.

Paisleys Outfitters, corner of Broomielaw and Jamaica Street, Glasgow – early 20th century
(J McCulloch Company, Caledonia postcard series)

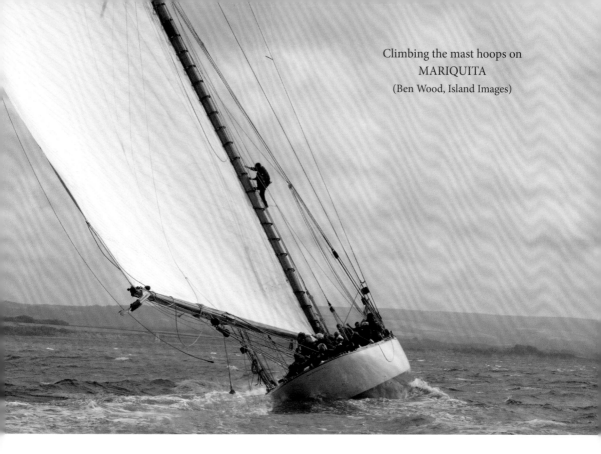

Climbing the mast hoops on
MARIQUITA
(Ben Wood, Island Images)

Danger

The work could be dangerous, especially on the big racing yachts. Although the cruising yachts had bulwarks, the out-and-out racers had neither bulwarks not guardrails. The decks were wet in heavy seas, but not as wet as the bowsprit end, where men were expected to work the jib sails without safety harnesses, secured only by a footrope and the strength of their arms. It was not unknown for these men to be washed away as the bow dipped into the waves.

During close quarters racing, collisions between the yachts were regular occurrences, with the long spars frequently fouling other boats. Indeed, some racing skippers sometimes deliberately arranged for their bowsprit or boom end to sweep over the stern of competing yachts to intimidate the opposition.

Climbing aloft was frequently required to set the topsail and clear fouled sheets or halyards, high above the deck. This climbing was performed without safety harnesses on masts without shrouds while the yacht raced along. The men simply climbed up the sail hoops around the mast. Working along the gaff from the mast was also performed without foot ropes or specific handholds as found on the spars of the big square-rigged commercial sailing vessels. Fatalities were not uncommon, even among experienced men. On the first appearance of James Pender's 23-Metre *Brynhild II* at the Thames racing in 1907, one of her mastheadsmen fell from aloft and was killed.

Mastheadsman
(Ben Wood, Island Images)

The sails and spars on the big yachts were huge and highly loaded. This extreme design led to things breaking from time to time, and when they did fail the forces released could be enormous. If a mast broke, the usual result was that the whole rig would go over the side, with falling spars presenting a risk to life and limb. *Lulworth* lost her rig when the mast failed 6 feet above the deck during a race on the Solent in 1927, and *Brynhild II* sank at Harwich Regatta in 1910 when her mast collapsed below deck and drove out through the bottom of the hull.

Even if nothing broke, the power in a large unsecured sail could injure or throw a man overboard as the sail and its sheets and blocks flogged violently. With the yacht moving at high speed, it often took too long to turn around and attempt recovery of the man in the water, although lifebelts were stowed at the stern of the boat for exactly this eventuality.

In June 1935 during one race on the Thames, *Velsheda* broke her boom, *Endeavour* lost her mast, and *Astra*'s spinnaker took the life of her steward.

Wreckage after dismasting of COLUMBIA - America's Cup Winner of 1899
(US Library of Congress)

YACHTS AND OWNERS – OVERVIEW

Cruising Yachts

Many of the Loch Broom men worked on sailing yachts which had the dual purpose of cruising as well as racing. They were outfitted with comfortable accommodation for their owners, and later examples may have had an auxiliary motor. Examples of this type of yacht would include *Roska* and *Thendara*, which are described in the next chapter.

The pure racing yachts would have no engine of any kind in order to maximise speed under sail, and to save weight the accommodation for the owner would be limited in comparison to the space available.

Racing Yachts

Metre Class Yachts

The International Rule of 1907 specified nine different classes; 5, 6, 7, 8, 9, 10, 12, 15 and 23 Metre. Later the 19-Metre was added. The class bracket for each yacht was defined by the output of mathematical formulae utilising input design parameters such as length, beam, freeboard and sail area.

For example, *Lulworth* qualified for the 23-Metre racing yacht class, which may seem strange considering her actual overall deck length was 37.2 metres (122 feet) or 46.30 metres (152 feet) including spars. However, the Rule did envisage a waterline length broadly equivalent to the rating, so that an original 8-Metre would have had a waterline length of close to 8 metres. The 24.6 metre actual waterline length of *Lulworth* was close to 23 metres, and so on.

Under the International Rule, the boats in any one class need not be identical but must all be designed with vital statistics which do not combine to exceed the formula limit for the class. The Rule was intended to encourage creativity in balancing designs to achieve the best overall performance, while also being comprehensive enough to eliminate loop holes which could result in impractical or extreme designs.

Especially in the larger sizes, the International Rule had emerged from a desire to create yachts with reasonable accommodation and to avoid special purpose "freaks", suitable only for racing. As a result, there were two elements to the rule; a "scantling" requirement which fixed minimum dimensions for all the structural components, and the rating calculation to measure the dimensions of the yacht hulls and their rigs on a common basis.

The descriptions in the following sections draw heavily on the writings of John Leather [9, 14].

23 Metre Class

The 23 metre boats carried approximately 10,000 square feet of sail without the spinnaker. They were about 110 feet long on deck, 80 feet waterline length and 21 feet beam. The first three built were Lipton's *Shamrock* of 1908 (not to be confused with the five America's Cup challengers of the same name), *White Heather II* (1907) and *Brynhild II* (1907).

Later examples included the Bermudan rigged *Cambria* (1928), *Astra* (1928) and *Candida* (1929). Together with the older *Britannia* (1893), *Lulworth* (1920) and the four 19-Metres, they formed the "Big Class". Some of these boats were later converted to race under J Class rules.

A 23-Metre boat cost about £12,000 fitted out, which was a huge sum around 1907. These boats required a crew of Skipper, Mate and 20 to 22 hands, and a season's racing would cost the owner about £5,000.

For comparison, up to around 1903 a 75ft long Zulu sailing fishing boat of 70 tonnes displacement could be built new for about £800 to £1,000, with another £400 or so for her fleet of drift nets. This type of boat was replaced around that time by the much more expensive 90ft steam drifter costing about £3,400 ready for sea with her fleet of nets.

Few West Coast fishermen could afford to build a new Zulu, and none could afford to order a steam drifter.

15 Metre Class

Compared to the 23-Metres, the 15-Metres required a much smaller crew of Skipper, Mate and only six or seven hands. They were also much cheaper to build, costing about £3,500, similar to the above-mentioned steam drifter. A typical 15-Metre might have a length on deck of 76 feet, a displacement of 40 tonnes and a sail area of 4,500 ft^2.

These smaller vessels formed the top sporting class of yacht in the UK from 1907 to 1914. The 1909 season saw a substantial increase in numbers, with seven new yachts built. Lochbroom men worked on *Jeano* (ex *Tritonia* of 1910) which belonged to this class.

The International Rule included minimum standards for accommodation. In the case of the 15-Metre class, the intent was that the owner could live on board for the season in reasonable comfort. The rule therefore required a "least height of cabin" of 6.23ft (1.90m), a "least breadth of floor" of 4.65ft (1.40m), four sleeping berths, and five sleeping "places" for the crew; and other details regarding lockers and toilets.

These 15-Metre boats made the annual circuit with the racing fleet to the regattas on the coasts of England, the east coast of Ireland and the Clyde. They were also capable of making North Sea summer passages to races on the west coast of Europe and the Baltic, but struggled in rough weather. They also suffered from limited space for storing the large wardrobe of different sails required for racing in a variety of conditions.

A total of twenty 15-Metre boats were built and raced in Britain, Spain, France and Germany. Two were ordered by crowned heads of Europe: *Hispania* for King Alfonso XIII of Spain in 1909, and *Isabel Alexandra* for Carl Gustav of Sweden in 1913. No more were built after 1918, and only four examples of this famous class are known to survive today; *Mariska, The Lady Anne, Hispania* and *Tuiga*.

15-Metre yachts racing at Kiel Regatta about 1912 with Zeppelin overhead

19 Metre Class

The 19-Metre class was introduced in 1911, as an attempted compromise between the large and expensive 23-Metre boats and the cheaper but limited 15-Metre boats.

During 1910 some owners in the 15-Metre class had concluded that a class midway between the 23 and 15-Metre yachts would offer improved seaworthiness for passage making, better accommodation for owners and guests, and provide the feeling of 'big yacht racing' without too great an increase in expense from the 15-Metres. A yacht of about 95ft overall length was considered desirable, and a 19-Metre rating class was eventually agreed for the summer of 1911.

By Christmas 1910 orders for four yachts were placed, three by experienced racing owners. The resulting yachts were typically 100 tons volumetric measurement and 70 tonnes displacement. They had a length on deck of about 95 feet and 62 feet waterline length, carrying 6,200 square feet of sail.

At about £6,000, the cost of a 19-Metre was not very much more than a 15-Metre racer and roughly half that of a 23-Metre.

They required a crew of a Skipper, Mate and 12 hands. Compared with a 23-Metre, the 19-Metre crew wage bill was about £13 less each week, then a considerable sum.

MARIQUITA under sail
(Ben Wood, Island Images)

Saloon on MARIQUITA
(image by Guido Cantini fotografo)

The 19-Metres were well regarded and performed well in competition. They would probably have developed into the largest racing class, but only the original four (*Mariquita, Octavia, Norada* and *Corona*) were completed before World War One brought an end to racing.

A Currie from Tighnabruaich was Skipper of *Mariquita*. Today this William Fife creation is the only survivor of the four, and was advertised for sale in 2015 with an asking price of 3.5 million Euros.

12 Metre Class

From 1924 to 1939 the smaller 12-Metre class provided much of the focus for UK yacht racing.

Typically 12-Metre class boats were 65 to 75 feet long overall (about 20 to 23 m). They were most often sloop-rigged, with masts roughly 85 feet (26 m) tall and a sail area of 2,000 square feet, excluding spinnaker.

In the inter-war period they cost about £4,500 new. Accommodation capacity was limited, but the boats required only a skipper and three hands to race, and so were more economical for owners. Although racing with 12-Metres was interrupted between 1939 and 1945, competition resumed after the war, and new 12-Metres continued to be built up to 1987.

The 12-Metre class boats are best known as the design used for the America's Cup from 1958 to 1987. When that competition resumed in 1958 there was a demand for cheaper vessels than the huge and expensive J-class yachts used in the 1930s. The 1987 America's Cup off Fremantle was the last occasion when the 12-Metre class was used (and the first time in 132 years that the New York Yacht Club did not defend the trophy).

8 Metre Class

The 8-Metre class was a medium size rating established under the International Rule. They were admitted as an Olympic class for the 1908 Olympics, and remained in the Olympics until 1936.

Before World War Two, the 8-Metres formed a very prestigious international yacht racing class, and they are still raced around the world. Between 1907 and 2008 approximately 500 8-Metre boats were built.

8-Metre boats are on average about 15 metres long overall and have a small cabin, theoretically allowing navigation from regatta to regatta.

6 Metre Class

The 6-Metre class was not the smallest rating established under the International Rule but was once the most popular. They were admitted as an Olympic class in 1908. These yachts were dayboats with an open cockpit for five people and no accommodation.

During their heyday in the 1920s and 1930s, 6-Metres were the most important international yacht racing class, attracting top sailors and designers to compete in events such as the Scandinavian Gold Cup and Olympics.

Clyde yachtsmen such as Herbert Thom, Fred and John Stephen, Maurice Clark (*Vadura*) and Arthur Young (*Thendara*) competed internationally in these boats during the 1920s and 1930s. Jackie "Buie" MacKenzie of Letters was a paid hand on Maurice Clark's 6-Metre *Vrana* during the 1939 season.

It was when the International Rule was revised in 1920 that the popularity of the 6-Metres as an international racing class really took off. However, under this Second International Rule (1920–33) the yachts went from less than 9.1 metres (30 feet) in overall length to almost 12 metres (40 feet), and the displacement increased by about 1 tonne. This led to criticism that the class had become too expensive and exclusive.

The smaller International 5.5-Metre class, introduced in 1949, quickly took over as the premier international racing class. The 6-Metres were dropped as an Olympic class after the 1952 Helsinki Games.

J-Class

The famous J boats were a class of large yacht which dominated the 1930s. These were based on a regulation method called the American Universal Rule, which divided yachts into classes according to sail area, displacement, length, and mast height. This resulted in an equivalent rating in feet, and the idea was that the yachts in a class would be evenly matched for racing.

Each class was notified by a letter of the alphabet – J being the largest and S the smallest. 'J' signified big yachts with a waterline length of between 76 and 87 feet, length overall of 120 feet, displacement of up to 160 tonnes, and an unrestricted sail plan.

The Bermudan mainsails of the J-Class were much smaller than the older gaff sails of the big yachts but still measured about 5,800 square feet. In cotton canvas this weighed about 1 tonne, and all hands were required to hoist and sheet these huge sails in a breeze.

Only ten J-Class yachts were built. Six of these were in the United States: *Enterprise, Weetamoe, Whirlwind* and *Yankee* in 1930, *Rainbow* in 1934 and *Ranger* in 1937. The four J-Class yachts built in the UK were *Shamrock V* in 1930, *Velsheda* in 1933, *Endeavour* in 1934 and *Endeavour II* in 1937. Except for *Velsheda*, all the J boats were built to challenge for the America's Cup.

Some older 23-Metre class boats were altered to meet the requirements of the J-Class, including *White Heather II, Britannia, Cambria, Candida* and *Astra* in the UK.

In their day, the J Class boats were the most technically advanced and admired yachts in the world. However, their reign lasted less than a decade. The 1937 America's Cup was the third and

British J Class Boats in 1934 (BRITANNIA, ASTRA, SHAMROCK V, CANDIDA)
(PHOTO © BEKEN)

last time J class yachts raced for the trophy. In 1938 the big class yachts did not fit out and never would again. The 12-Metre class had become popular by then as they were "only" 70ft long and much less costly than the J-Class.

All the American examples were scrapped and only three of the British J boats survived. However, fascination with the class has persisted, and *Endeavour* was the first to be fully restored in the 1980s, with *Velsheda* and *Shamrock V* following. With no other original boats to restore, people have resorted to building replicas, beginning with the American yacht *Ranger*, a copy of which was launched in 2003. Some owners are now commissioning yachts from 1930s plans for J class designs that were never built at the time.

The modern boats cost around £13m. Running expenses are around £1m to £2m per year, driven by items such as sails costing around £100,000 for a single genoa.

Steam Yachts

The yachtsmen were not employed only on pure sailing vessels. Loch Broom men also worked on a number of steam yachts, including *Zara, Ariana, Oriana, Sheila* and others.

Steam yachts became a practical proposition in the 1840s and remained popular with wealthy individuals and heads of state into the early 20th century. The first steam powered British royal yacht was the *Victoria & Albert* of 1843 and the first example in the USA was shipping magnate Cornelius Vanderbilt's *North Star* of 1854.

Private steam yachts of this type were capable of long sea voyages, and several of them did cover long distances. A typical season would involve summer cruising in Scotland, Norway and the Baltic, followed by a winter in the Mediterranean.

This was not without its risks in those days without modern navigational aids. In 1889 Sir John Fowler's *Southern Cross* ran aground on Skye. In July 1901 the steam yacht *Monsoon* struck a rock near the mouth of Little Loch Broom when on passage from Stornoway to Ullapool in a thick fog. The *Athena*, another steam yacht, proceeded from Ullapool to assist but it was feared that the *Monsoon* would become a total loss.

Many owners of steam yachts also owned racing sailing yachts. In such cases the steam yacht often acted as a tender or tug for the racer and provided living accommodation for the owner.

Scotland was heavily involved in the production of these symbols of wealth and power. G L Watson (1851 – 1904) of Glasgow was a prominent designer of steam yachts. Ramage & Ferguson at Leith were leading builders, and Clydeside yards also produced these vessels in large numbers. Clyde yards are reported to have built 190 steam yachts between 1830 and 1935, while Scotts of Greenock alone built 23 steam yachts between 1876 and 1904.

A later NORTH STAR owned
by the Vanderbilt family
(US Library of Congress)

They were usually designed to produce a similar hull appearance to the sailing clippers of the mid-1800s, with a clipper bow and bowsprit, and a low, graceful sheer line. Their fine lines and heavy displacement gave them good seakeeping characteristics. Propulsion came from one or two steam engines, of compound type, or later, in very large yachts, triple expansion type or turbines.

Steam yachts usually carried some masts and rigging for sails, originally as a serious method of auxiliary propulsion, but later more for the sake of appearance. There was a limited network of coaling stations in existence when steam power came to the fore at sea, and the early steam auxiliary yachts were capable of covering long distances between coaling stations under a full sailing rig. When not in steam, the funnel on some of the early steam auxiliary yachts could be lowered and the propeller feathered to reduce drag.

Yachts of the Loch Broom Men

The yachts on which the Loch Broom men served seem to have been in the top rank, certainly of the cruiser-racer variety. Although not usually out-and-out racers, they included the work of the most famous British designers and builders, such as Alfred Mylne and William Fife. Many were large, and so available to only the wealthiest and keenest owners.

The following tables summarise the main features of the yachts on which Loch Broom men were known to have worked in the early 20th century, and which are covered to some extent in this book. Other vessel names associated with Loch Broom men include; *Iris, Maimie, Mimosa, Rinancy* and *Sabine*.

List of Sailing/Auxiliary Yachts

Name	Type when built	T.M. tons	Length	Designer	Year Built	Builder	Status
Astra	Bermudan cutter (23m)	164	115ft	Charles Nicholson	1928	Camper & Nicholson	Restored and sailing
Ceol Mara	Auxiliary ketch	63	70ft	WG McBryde	1929	James Miller, St Monance	
Eileen	Gaff ketch (Bermudan mizzen)	94	84ft	William Fife	1929	Fife, Fairlie	Restored and sailing as *Belle Aventure*
Fedoa	Gaff ketch	33	58ft	Alfred Mylne	1927	Bute Slip Dock	Destroyed by fire 2016
Fiumara	Gaff ketch	77	79ft	Alfred Mylne	1934	Stephen, Linthouse	Restored and sailing as *Alinda V*
Florinda	Gaff yawl (ketch)	135	101ft	Builder	1873	Camper & Nicholson	
Gleniffer	Gaff schooner	496	185ft	GL Watson	1899	D&W Henderson, Glasgow	
Hotspur	Gaff yawl	102	76.5ft	unknown	1874	At Cowes	Houseboat at West Mersea
Jeano (ex Tritonia)	Gaff cutter (15-Metre)	51	75ft	Alfred Mylne	1910	Robertson, Sandbank	Trace lost in Brazil, 1980s
Kentra	Gaff ketch	87	82ft	William Fife	1923	Fife, Fairlie	Restored and sailing
Lulworth (ex Terpsichore)	Gaff cutter (23-Metre)	186	122ft	Herbert White	1920	White, Southampton	Restored and sailing
Mafalda	Yawl	17	41ft	W Watkins	1891	Watkins, London	
Mariella	Bermudan yawl	74	79ft	Alfred Mylne	1938	Fife, Fairlie	Restored and sailing

List of Sailing/Auxiliary Yachts (cont.)

Name	Type when built	T.M. tons	Length	Designer	Year Built	Builder	Status
Molin	Bermudan cutter	13	33ft	Builder	1930	RS Burt, Falmouth	
Morna	Gaff ketch	22	48ft	Peter Dickie	1920	Dickie, Tarbert	Restored and sailing
Oceana	Gaff schooner	206	106ft	unknown	1880	Hansen, Cowes	Wrecked at Tiree, 1949
Panope	Gaff schooner	120	97ft	Alfred Mylne	1928	Camper & Nicholson	Lost in hurricane, 1970s
Pelagia	Gaff yawl	41	72ft	Fred Shepherd	1903	White, Southampton	Discovered in the Caribbean in need of restoration
Roska	Gaff ketch	62	75ft	Alfred Mylne	1930	Bute Slip Dock	Sailing as Arosa for Spanish Navy (school ship)
Satellite	Gaff yawl	63	68ft	Fife	1852	Fife, Fairlie	
The Ketch	Gaff ketch	111	87ft	William Fife	1906	Fife, Fairlie	
Thendara (ex Brada)	Gaff yawl	48	61ft	Builder	1901	Stow, Shoreham	
Thendara	Gaff ketch	147	105ft	Alfred Mylne	1937	Stephen, Linthouse	Restored and sailing
Uldra	Cruising cutter	56	64.5ft	William Fife	1905	Fife, Fairlie	
Vadura	Gaff yawl	109	91.5ft	Alfred Mylne	1926	Stephen, Linthouse	
Valentine	Gaff yawl	20	50ft	AR Luke	1902	WG Luke, Hamble	Afloat, California
Vida VI (built as Rose)	Gaff yawl (originally)	80	73ft	William Fife	1906	Fife, Fairlie	
Waratah	Schooner	19	42ft	Builder	1877	MacKenzie, Little Loch Broom	

List of Steam or Motor Yachts

Name	Type when built	T.M. tons	Length on deck	Designer	Year Built	Builder	Status
Anna Marie	Motor yacht	344	145ft	Builder	1930	JL Thornycroft, Southampton	Lost in RN service, WW2
Ariana	Steam yacht	347	155ft	Builder	1902	Ramage & Ferguson, Leith	
Carraig	Steam yacht	64	84ft	Builder	1910	John Reid, Whiteinch, Glasgow	
Golden Eagle	Steam yacht	455	159ft	GL Watson	1899	Ramage & Ferguson, Leith	
Medea	Steam yacht	137	134ft	Frederic Stephen, Mylne	1904	Stephen, Linthouse, Glasgow	Preserved in San Diego
Narcissus	Steam yacht	816	222ft		1904	Fairfield, Glasgow	Lost in RN service, WW2
Norseman (3 off)	Steam yacht	202 325 521	115ft 138ft 160ft	St Clare John Byrne	1877 1890 1898	Various	
Oriana	Steam yacht	172	100ft	Builder	1896	Charles Connell, Glasgow	
Ottawa	Motor cutter	34	54ft	GL Watson	1912	McGruer, Clynder	
Rionnag na Mara	Steam yacht	310	153ft	Builder	1886	John Reid, Port Glasgow	
Sheila	Steam yacht	80	79ft	Builder	1904	W. White, Cowes	
Sonamara	Motor schooner	35	48ft	Builder	1936	Hugh MacLean, Renfrew	
Southern Cross (3 off)	Steam yachts	119 332 71	98.5ft 161ft 82ft	Various	1876 1878 1886	Various	
Thendara (ex *Aloha*)	Motor yacht	94	90ft	Charles Nicholson	1924	Camper & Nicholson	
Zara	Steam yacht	516	178ft	GL Watson	1895	Ailsa Shipbuilding, Troon	

Distinguishing Flags of Selected Yachts
(Lloyds Register of Yachts, 1925, 1937)

Glasgow Area Owners

Details of the individual owners and their lives are given in the following chapter, but the table opposite summarises key dates and business interests of the most prominent Clydeside owners for whom the Loch Broom sailors worked. Many of these owners died in close succession in the years around 1950.

Key Dates of Glasgow Yacht Owners

Vessel(s)	Type when built	Owner	Years as Owner	Years Living	Business interests
Ariana	Steam yacht	Thomas Dunlop	1924 to 1938	1855 to 1938	Ship owner
Carraig	Steam yacht	James Lithgow	1924 to 1952	1883 to 1952	Ship builder
Ceol Mara	Motor yacht	William Lorimer	1948 to 1954	1876 to 1954	North British Locomotive Works
Eileen	Gaff ketch	Louis Vandalle Fulton	1929 to 1934	1879 to 1934	Steel merchant and ship owner
Fedoa	Gaff ketch	Joseph MacLay	1934 to 1951	1857 to 1951	Ship owner
Fedoa	Gaff ketch	William Wordie	1927 to 1934	1884 to 1952	Haulage, transportation
Fiumara	Gaff ketch		1934 to 1952		
Gleniffer	Gaff schooner	James Coats Junior	1899 to 1912	1841 to 1912	Member of Coats thread family, Paisley
Golden Eagle	Steam yacht	William Raeburn	1925 to 1934	1850 to 1934	Ship owner
Kentra	Gaff ketch	Barclay Hogarth	1936 to 1951	1878 to 1951	Ship owner
Mariella	Bermudan yawl	Ronald Teacher	1939 to 1969	1900 to 1976	Whisky distilling
Oriana	Steam yacht	Claud Allan	1926 to 1939 or later	1871 to 1945	Ship owner
Roska	Gaff ketch	Andrew MacGeorge	1930 to 1959	1887 to 1959	Stockbroker
Valentine	Gaff yawl		1926 to 1930		
Sheila	Steam yacht	Robert S Allan	1923 to 1932	1857 to 1932	Ship owner
Thendara (ex Brada)	Gaff yawl	Arthur Young	1923 to 1950	1899 to 1950	Templeton carpet firm
Thendara	Motor yacht				
Thendara (1937)	Gaff ketch				
Vadura	Gaff yawl	Maurice Clark	1926 to 1940	1892 to 1941	Ship owner, member of Clark thread family, Paisley
Vida VI	Gaff yawl (originally)	William Wylie	1920 to 1935	1856 to 1939	Furniture, outfitting, undertaking
Zara	Steam yacht	Peter Coats	1895 to 1913	1842 to 1913	Member of Coats thread family, Paisley

INDIVIDUAL YACHTS
AND OWNERS

Anna Marie

The Yacht

Anna Marie was a large motor yacht, originally built in 1930 by JL Thornycroft of Southampton for Danish industrialist Valdemar Graae. He owned her for a very short time before she was acquired by prominent Liverpool solicitor and businessman WE Corlett in 1931 and renamed *Llys Helig*.

The vessel passed through several owners in short order. In 1933 she was sold and renamed *Northern Lights*, and then bought in 1935 by the Earl of Dudley who reverted to her original name. Another ownership change occurred in 1938 before the yacht was taken over by the Royal Navy in 1939.

In naval service she worked on anti-submarine duties, and was initially known as *HMS Anna Marie* (FY 004), and later as *HMS Torrent*. The vessel struck a mine and sank off Falmouth in April 1941.

Anna Marie was 145ft length overall, 136ft waterline length with a beam of 23.9ft. She had a Thames measurement of 344 tons and was powered by two Gardner engines.

Loch Broom Men

There are few photographs of the *Anna Marie* or her Loch Broom crew. One which survives and is reproduced in the next chapter is of Kenny "Skene" MacKenzie. This shows him in his yachting jersey, standing beside a large motor car, presumably the owner's.

Ariana

The Yacht

Ariana was a steam yacht (although schooner rigged) of 155 feet length and 22 feet beam, with

Motor Yacht ANNA MARIE in the Solent, 1934
(Supermarine factory in the background)
(Alamy)

an engine of 82hp, built of steel in 1902 by Ramage & Ferguson of Leith. Before World War One this vessel belonged to a Mr George Clark and was based at Leith. For most of the 1920s and 1930s she was owned by Sir Thomas Dunlop of Glasgow.

Ramage & Fergusons were specialists in steam yacht design and construction, active from 1877. The yard was taken over by Henry Robb of Leith in 1934.

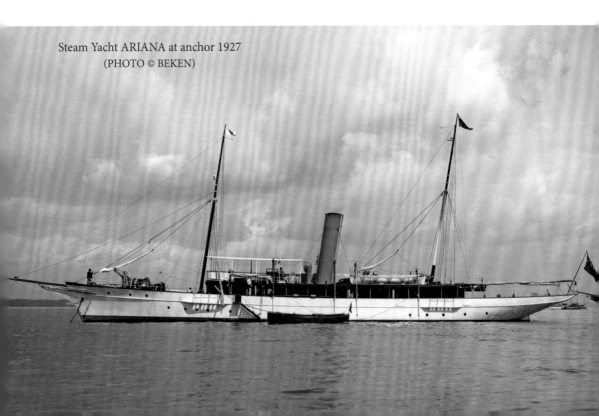

Steam Yacht ARIANA at anchor 1927
(PHOTO © BEKEN)

The Owner – Thomas Dunlop

Thomas Dunlop (1855 – 1938) was a Scottish businessman, a partner in his father's shipping company, and later a director of the Royal Bank of Scotland and the Scottish Union and National Insurance Company. In 1914, he became Lord Provost of Glasgow and was created a baronet in 1916 due to this position. He was the son of Thomas Dunlop (1831–1893), founder of the shipping company Thomas Dunlop & Sons of Wellington Street, Glasgow, later known as the Queen Line.

Thomas Dunlop senior was a provision and grain merchant who bought his first ship in 1868. He eventually owned 14 sailing ships, one of which was the iron barque *Clan MacLeod* of 1874, which survives today as the *James Craig* in Sydney, Australia. In 1878 Dunlop changed his ship naming prefix from "Clan" to "Queen" to avoid confusion with the ships of Cayzer-Irvine's Clan Line. In 1883 he took delivery of his first steamship. The line traded until 1956 when the last ship was sold and the company wound up.

In 1937, shortly before his death, Sir Thomas Dunlop was commodore of the Royal Clyde Yacht Club and the Cruising Club.

Three-masted barque JAMES CRAIG (ex CLAN MACLEOD) at Sydney, 2007
(image by Alphamuchi from Wikimedia Commons)

Loch Broom Men

Several Loch Broom men were employed on *Ariana,* including Hugh MacKenzie and Alec (Lally) MacKenzie. The photograph shows Lally (Alec Mackenzie) wearing an *Ariana* jersey while visiting friends onboard the *Roska.* Since William MacGregor joined the *Roska* in 1937 and Thomas Dunlop died in 1938, this helps to date the photograph. An earlier *Ariana* crew photograph from the 1920s is reproduced in the section on *Pelagia.*

Astra

The Yacht

Astra is a historically important survivor from 1928. She is a big Bermudan rigged cutter, built for Mortimer Singer, son of the sewing machine tycoon, and owner of the gaff cutter *Lulworth.*

She was designed by Charles Nicholson for the 23-Metre class of the Second International Rule, but later modified to race under J Class rules. The Camper & Nicholson yard at Gosport constructed the hull of Honduras mahogany planking on steel frames, with yellow pine decks. *Astra* is 115ft long overall, 75ft waterline length, with a breadth of 20ft. These dimensions gave her a Thames tonnage of 164, and a displacement of 140 tonnes.

Lally (Alec MacKenzie) on right, wearing ARIANA jersey together with crew on ROSKA (William MacGregor in background) (MacGregor photo)

Her debut season in 1928 was the first real test of the new Bermudan rig against the older gaff rig. *Astra* did not perform as well as expected, largely due to a handicapping system which did not favour her. However, the new rig proved much simpler and faster to handle, with fewer crew.

New ratings were adopted for the 1929 season, and the Bermudan yachts were allowed to increase the height of their masts. *Astra* began the season well with four victories from five races, but Mortimer Singer died before the Clyde regatta, and *Astra* withdrew from competition. After a few months she was bought by Sir Howard Frank, head of the Knight, Frank & Rutley property agency. Frank raced *Astra* in the summer of 1930, and then sold her to Hugh Paul of the Ipswich milling family, who had previously owned *Sumurun.*

Paul intended racing *Astra* under the J Class rule in the 1931 season, and she was adapted accordingly. Her draft was reduced, and her mast was changed for a taller, hollow wooden design. Before the start of the 1933 season, Hugh Paul decided on further modifications to remedy the disadvantage of her smaller size; increasing her waterline length by 2m.

By 1936, only a reduced fleet was competing, and *Astra* benefitted from a favourable rating allowance. The purpose built J Class boats had to give *Astra* 8.8 seconds every mile, and this often proved enough to ensure her victory in light winds.

Post War Owners

Hugh Paul died after World War Two, and in 1948 his executors sold the vessel. She was soon sold on again, and her owner in 1951 and 1952 was Commander HG Dobbs (RN, retired). *Astra* was then sold to Count Andrea Matarazzo, a Brazilian coffee baron, based in Naples, where she arrived in the spring of 1953.

Astra remained in Italy for the following decades but was eventually retired and laid up in a shed at Salerno. In spring 1982, Giancarlo Bussei, a cousin of Gianni Agnelli, discovered *Astra* and a long restoration began at the Beconcini yard in La Spezia. *Astra* went back to sea in July 1988 and moved under power to Antibes where her 50m high mast was fitted. She spent the first cruising season of her new life in the Mediterranean, and the following year crossed the Atlantic to meet former J class competitors *Endeavour* and *Shamrock V* in Newport, Rhode Island.

Giancarlo Bussei kept *Astra* for two more seasons, and sold her in 1993 to Giuseppe Degennaro, a well-known Italian yacht racer. She moved to Greece in the summer of 2012.

Loch Broom Men

Although not strictly from Lochbroom, Roddy MacLean from Inverasdale worked on the *Astra* and later lived in Ullapool. His details are given in a later chapter.

Carraig

The Yacht

Carraig was a modestly sized steam yacht designed and built in 1910 by John Reid of Glasgow. She was 84ft long overall, 74ft waterline length and 14ft beam. Thames measurement was 64 tons.

She was owned from 1924 to 1952 by the Port Glasgow shipbuilder James Lithgow. *Carraig* was purchased mainly to give access to Ormsary Estate on Jura which James Lithgow bought in 1922.

The Owner – James Lithgow

James Lithgow (1883-1952) was a prominent Scottish shipbuilder and industrialist. He played a major role in restructuring the British shipbuilding industry in the 1930s, in addition to holding important positions supervising industrial production during both World Wars.

ASTRA sailing downwind with spinnaker
(Alamy)

His father William was a partner in the Port Glasgow shipbuilding firm of Russell & Co, where James and his brother Henry were apprenticed and later made partners. This firm was famous for its early 20th century production of many of the last square-rigged sailing cargo ships. William died in 1908 and his two sons took control of the company. In 1919 they restructured the partnership of Russell & Co. into Lithgows Ltd.

Henry focused on the day-to-day business of shipbuilding, which enabled James to take a more external and public role. During World War One, James served with a howitzer battery on the Western Front and was awarded the Military Cross. In May 1917 he returned to England and was appointed Director of Merchant Shipbuilding with responsibility to ensure that production targets were achieved. This was his first step into public life and introduced him to many influential people. Early in World War Two, Winston Churchill appointed James as Controller of Merchant Shipbuilding and Repair and as a Lord Commissioner of the Admiralty. Lithgow also had a brief responsibility for tank production and worked with Harold Macmillan on the Industrial Capacity Committee of the Production Council.

Between the wars, National Shipbuilders Securities (NSS) was formed in 1930 to remove excess shipbuilding capacity during the Great Depression. In the decade to 1939, NSS purchased and closed around a third of British shipbuilding capacity, with James Lithgow as Chairman seen as the public face and architect of the scheme. In contrast to this unpopular role, he served as chairman of the Scottish National Development Council and played a leading role in the promotion of Hillington Industrial Estate and the Empire Exhibition of 1938 in Glasgow.

The Lithgow's own shipbuilding business embarked on a process of acquisition and expansion, purchasing other yards and adopting vertical integration by involvement in coal mining and steelmaking. At the time of his death in 1952, Sir James Lithgow controlled the largest privately owned shipyard in the world. Up to that point Lithgows had a reputation for efficient production.

James Lithgow was very close to his brother Henry and they enjoyed shooting grouse and deer together at their estates on the island of Jura. Henry died in 1948 and this was a severe blow to James. Four months after Henry's death, he suffered a thrombosis and stroke from which he never fully recovered. James Lithgow died at Langbank on the Clyde in February 1952 and is buried at Ormsary.

The company the brothers had built up slowly declined along with the rest of the British shipbuilding industry, and in 1967 Lithgows merged with the neighbouring Scotts Shipbuilding and Engineering Company. During the 1970s Scott Lithgow engaged in a technology transfer arrangement with the Korean Hyundai Heavy Industries which allowed that company to enter and later dominate the world shipbuilding business. The combined Scott Lithgow was nationalised as part of British Shipbuilders in 1977, then purchased by Trafalgar House in 1984, and ceased to trade in 1993.

Above: Edward MacKenzie
and Angie "Allan" MacKenzie
of the CARRAIG, c. 1950
(Ullapool Museum)

Left: Port Glasgow
Shipyards, early 1960s

Loch Broom Men

Edward Bayley MacKenzie from Letters was employed on the *Carraig* for many years. A young Angie "Allan" MacKenzie also worked on her briefly before 1950.

Ceol Mara

The Yacht

Ceol Mara was a twin screw auxiliary ketch built by James Miller of St Monans in 1929. James Miller was a yard more normally employed in the construction of wooden fishing vessels but was capable of building yachts. The Clyde based WG McBryde was the designer.

The yacht was 70ft long overall, 55ft waterline length and had a beam of 16ft, giving a Thames measurement of 63 tons. She was originally fitted with two 6 cylinder Gleniffer paraffin engines, which were later replaced by Perkins diesels.

The Owner – William Lorimer

During the 1930s the yacht was based on the east coast of Scotland. In 1939 *Ceol Mara* was owned by Lord Trent and based at Granton. She was taken over by the Royal Navy during the Second World War.

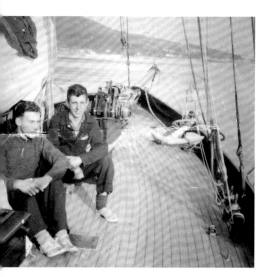

Eric "Nelson" MacKenzie on right –
onboard CEOL MARA in the Holy
Loch on the Clyde in 1947
(Eric MacKenzie photo)

In the post-war period when Eric "Nelson" MacKenzie was employed, the *Ceol Mara* was owned by Mr Lorimer of the North British Locomotive Company, based in Springburn, Glasgow.

William Lorimer (1876 - 1954) spent his entire career with this business. He was the eldest son of Sir William Lorimer, a senior partner in the Glasgow locomotive building business of Dubs and Co. This firm was founded in 1863, and forty years later was one of the companies which became part of the North British Locomotive Company.

Shortly after the formation of the North British Locomotive Company, William Lorimer was appointed a managing director, and in 1935 he became Chairman. He continued in that office until his retirement in 1946. He was afflicted by blindness from 1926 but was still able to handle the details and complexities concerned with a large business.

Loch Broom Men

After World War Two a young Eric MacKenzie (b. 1932) worked briefly onboard the *Ceol Mara*.

Eileen (now Belle Aventure)

The Yacht

The Fulton family owned a series of Fife designed and built boats named *Eileen* (84ft, 1929), *Eileen 2* (the 60ft "*wee Eileen*") and *Eilean* (70ft, 1936). All three are still in existence.

Their origins lie in 1928 when Sir Louis Vandalle Fulton (1879-1934) requested a proposal from William Fife III for a new yacht. Fife presented the plans of *Eileen*, a 60ft Bermuda rigged yawl/cutter, very similar to another boat he was about to complete for Norman Clark-Neill, the *Maryk*. Construction commenced on this design, but Fulton changed his mind and asked for something larger. Fife then proposed a much larger ketch, which was accepted by Fulton and delivered at Fairlie in June 1929 as the 84ft *Eileen* (yard number 772) This boat sails today as the beautifully restored *Belle Aventure*. His sons Robert and James took the smaller *Eileen* (yard number 769).

The big *Eileen* was an auxiliary ketch, constructed with two-inch teak planking over heavy oak frames. She has a length of 84'6" on deck (94ft over spars), with a beam of 17.7ft. Her motor was a 9hp Bergius (Kelvin), tiny even by the standards of the day, and for a boat of this size only useful in a complete absence of wind. In modern times she has a 180hp diesel.

Originally built with 3,750 ft² of sail set on a compromise design of gaff rigged mainsail and Bermudan mizzen, her second owner asked Fife to change her sail plan to that of a 3,000 ft² Bermudan ketch in 1937. Her name was also changed to *Alison*, then *My Lady of Aros*, until finally she was re-christened *Belle Aventure* by a new European owner in the 1960s.

This yacht has sailed throughout the world exploring Europe, North Africa, South America, the Caribbean and Bermuda, the Eastern USA, Tahiti and the South Pacific, as well as the Philippines, Australia and New Zealand. In recent years she has returned to the Clyde as part of the regular Fife regattas.

The fact that she has continuously maintained her Lloyds A1 classification status over ninety years of intensive sailing is a testament to the fine craftsmanship of Fife's shipwrights and the meticulous maintenance by her dedicated owners and crew.

The Owners – Fulton family

The Fultons were steel merchants and ship owners from Greenock, Scotland and members of the Royal Gourock Yacht Club.

This family became prominent in the iron and steel trading firm of P MacCallum & Sons after a James Fulton bought into the company. The firm of P MacCallum had developed from an 18th century hardware business supplying the expanding ship and boat building industry on the Lower Clyde. From making nails and spikes, the firm expanded into the bulk iron trade, winning contracts for the supply of iron plate, which was replacing wood as the prime shipbuilding material in the middle of the 19th century. By 1870 they supplied all the Greenock and Port Glasgow shipyards and engineering works. In 1869 Thomas MacCallum died suddenly and his nephew, John Lang, became a partner. He ran the business with the help of James Fulton, his head clerk, who bought the last MacCallum shares in 1874.

The Lang and Fulton partnership began to diversify into shipping, forming a new company in 1876 to manage their shipping interests. John Lang and James Fulton expanded the ship owing business and by 1912 they owned 13 sailing ships and managed an additional eight. Before World War One Lang & Fulton also began a profitable investment in steamships, building up a fleet of 29 vessels. The ships were all named with the prefix 'Ard' such as *Ardglen, Ardgoil* and *Ardgarval.*

When Louis Fulton died in 1934 his sons James and Robert sold the 84ft *Eileen* and took delivery of the 70ft *Eilean* auxiliary cruising ketch built by Fife in 1936 (yard number 822). Both brothers failed to return from World War Two. Robert (b. 1912), an artillery major, was killed in Tunisia in 1943 and James (b. 1909), a RN lieutenant-commander, lost his life during a U-boat attack in the Arctic.

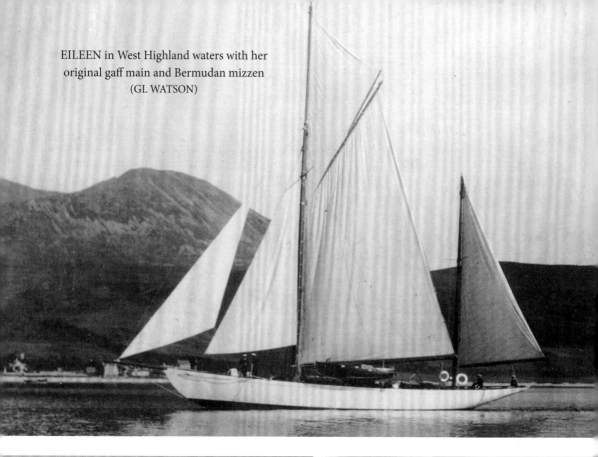

EILEEN in West Highland waters with her
original gaff main and Bermudan mizzen
(GL WATSON)

EILEEN as BELLE
AVENTURE
(Alamy)

The Builder - Fife

William Fife III, also known as Wm. Fife, Jr (1857–1944), was the third generation of a boatbuilding dynasty based at Fairlie on the Ayrshire coast of the Firth of Clyde [6]. His father and grandfather were William Fife II (1821–1902) and William Fife I (1785–1865), respectively. The family business operated from a yard in an unpromising location above the shallow shelving village beach.

Fife III began building yachts in 1890 and soon surpassed the achievements of his father and grandfather, becoming known as one of the top yacht designers of the day. Fife designed the America's Cup challengers *Shamrock I* (1899) and *Shamrock III* (1903) for grocery and tea magnate Sir Thomas Lipton. After the creation of the first International Rule in 1906, Fife became a prolific designer of Metre boats, designing and building several successful 15-Metre and 19-Metre yachts in the years leading up to the Great War. Between 1907 and 1913, William Fife III designed eight of the twenty 15-Metre yachts built.

The Fairlie yard was known for the extremely high quality of its workmanship. It was said that a razor blade could not be inserted in any joint onboard a Fife built yacht [1]. Fife III died in 1944, never having married, and is buried in Largs, Ayrshire. The yard was operated for some years after William Fife's death by his nephew and built some ring-net fishing boats before finally closing.

Fife designed 1903 America's Cup
challenger SHAMROCK III
(US Library of Congress)

Left: Launch of the 19-Metre MARIQUITA in 1911 at Fairlie – Floating Launch Dock on left
(photo by W Coutts Hampton, Largs)

Right: A very young Lally (Alec MacKenzie) - on right - near the mizzen mast on EILEEN
Sandy "Bain" MacKenzie on left, Johnny MacDonald, Torridon in centre
(Ullapool Museum)

Left: Belle Aventure
(ex EILEEN) at Rhu
Marina, Clyde
(Alamy)
Note same skylight
detail forward of the
mizzen mast as in old
photograph

Right: Looking aft on
EILEEN under sail
(Ullapool Museum)

Loch Broom Men

Lally (Alec MacKenzie) worked on this vessel. Duncan MacPherson from Gairloch (grandfather of Diyanne Ross, Coigach) was also a crewman.

Fedoa

The Yacht

Fedoa was a modestly sized ketch 58ft on deck and 40ft waterline length, 13ft beam and 8ft draft. She was launched in 1926 and completed in 1927. This boat was Alfred Mylne design No. 309, and was built at his own Bute Slip Dock Company for Colonel William Wordie OBE, of Glasgow and Greenock.

FEDOA
(Eric MacKenzie photo)

Fedoa was destroyed by fire in 2016, along with 32 other yachts, while nearing the end of an extensive restoration on the Isle of Wight.

First Owner – William Wordie

Col. Wordie (1884 - 1952) was Chairman of Wordie & Co, Scotland's largest road hauliers and carriers of the time. The firm had been established at Stirling by his great-grandfather John in the early 19th century, and became very successful with the expansion of the railway network in the mid-1800s. In 1874 William's father John inherited an enormous business based on horse-drawn transport. He moved the family to Glasgow, where he built the family home at 52 Cleveden Drive in the West End around 1880.

During the First World War William Wordie served in the Royal Army Service Corps (Territorial Force) and became a Colonel. He raced and cruised *Fedoa* around the West Coast of Scotland until 1934 when she was replaced by the larger *Fiumara*. During the 1930s (after he sold *Fedoa*) Col. Wordie moved from Cleveden Drive to the nearby Kingsborough Gardens, Hyndland.

After the Second World War, Wordie & Co was nationalised and became part of British Road Services. The extensive city centre stables required for the pre-war horse-drawn business were converted to other purposes.

William's brother James Mann Wordie was a successful academic who studied geology and accompanied Shackleton on the famous *Endurance* expedition to the Antarctic. After war service in the Royal Artillery, he returned to academia and ran several privately-financed Arctic explorations from his base at St John's College, Cambridge.

Later Owners – Joseph MacLay and Others

Fedoa's second owner was Baron Joseph Paton MacLay (1857 - 1951) of Kilmacolm near Glasgow. MacLay had formed a shipping company with Thomas Walker Macintyre in 1885.

The company was started with six small steamers to operate tramp services. By 1896 the company owned 33 ships and concentrated on the coal trade to Algoa Bay (South Africa) and the ore trade from the Mediterranean. Joseph MacLay was the Chairman of MacLay and MacIntyre Shipping Company until he retired in 1905 when the business was run by Walter McIntyre. The last two ships were sold in 1960 and the company dissolved.

MacLay became a town councillor and magistrate in Glasgow. In 1916 he was appointed Minister of Shipping by the wartime government. Two of MacLay's sons were killed in the First World War and the University of Glasgow's MacLay Hall is named in their memory. In 1921 MacLay and his wife Martha gifted this building in Park Terrace overlooking Kelvingrove Park for use as a student hall of residence.

This act may have inspired his neighbour Laurence MacBrayne (c. 1867 - 1941), who in 1923 also gifted his former family home at 11 Park Circus Place to the University for a hall of residence, "*with a preference for students from the Western Highlands and Islands*". It was named MacBrayne Hall in memory of his father, the shipowner David MacBrayne (1818-1907).

Joseph MacLay kept *Fedoa* from the 1930s until his death in the early 1950s. By 1955 she was across the Atlantic in Antigua.

Loch Broom Men

Several of the "Nelson" family of Lochside MacKenzies worked on the *Fedoa*, including John who was employed as the Skipper.

Another John MacKenzie (Onorach) was also employed as Skipper by William Wordie in the years 1926-28. This would have included the *Fedoa*, which was new in 1927.

Fiumara

Men in working gear at the bow of FEDOA - John "Nelson" MacKenzie on left with another Lochsider (Eric MacKenzie photo)

The Yacht

Fiumara was a big gaff ketch completed in May 1934 to a design by Alfred Mylne (design number 351). She was slightly larger than Mylne's *Roska* design of 1930, with length over spars 91ft, length on deck 78.75ft, waterline length 55.6ft, beam 17ft and draft 10.3ft. She was completed with a 36hp engine.

This yacht was built for William Wordie as a step up from his previous *Fedoa*, also designed by Mylne. He kept *Fiumara* until his death in 1952.

Fiumara was one of two similar cruising yachts built in 1934, the other being *Albyn* (completed in June 1934 for tobacco magnate Robert French). Both yachts were built at the Stephen of Linthouse shipyard in Glasgow, with composite construction of steel framing and timber planking.

The costs recorded in Stephen's records for *Fiumara* (yard number 539) are as follows [13];
- – Invoiced price £10,250 (before £900 deduction applied)
- – Hull materials £4,019 and hull labour £2,990
- – Overheads contribution £0, and net profit £2,341

Fiumara was laid up at Port Bannatyne on Bute during World War Two. She beat *Thendara* in the first post-war race from Hunters Quay to Tarbert, Loch Fyne. As well as Col. Wordie, the crew on that occasion consisted of Captain Dan MacFarlane from Port Bannatyne, John and Iain Martin from Harris, Dan Urquhart (steward) from Ullapool and a young Angie "Allan" MacKenzie from Letters, Loch Broom.

Fiumara is still afloat, renamed *Alinda V*, and has been restored by Southampton Yacht Services.

The Builder – Stephen, Linthouse

Alexander Stephen and Sons Limited, often referred to simply as Alex Stephens or just Stephens, was a shipbuilding company based at Linthouse, Glasgow, on the south bank of the River Clyde.

The Stephen yard's usual business was large steel ships, but the owners were considerate employers and took on the relatively trivial *Fiumara* and *Albyn* work to keep skilled carpenters employed at a time of low activity in the Clyde shipyards. In 1932, when the sixth generation of Stephens, represented by Alexander Murray Stephen (1892-1974), took over as Chairman and Managing Director, there was no work in his yard or most others in the country due to the worldwide economic depression.

The best-known example was John Brown, Clydebank where all work on building *Queen Mary* (then Hull Number 534) was halted on 11th December 1931. Some 3,000 John Brown shipyard workers were laid off and work did not restart until May 1934.

The Stephen's care for their workers was demonstrated by the creation of a welfare department, providing a large works canteen and facilities for sport and recreation, including Coila Park (ten acres of land at Shieldhall).

FIUMARA at Torquay
Coronation Regatta 1937
(PHOTO © BEKEN)

The first Alexander Stephen had begun wooden shipbuilding at Burghead on the Moray Firth, in about 1750. The business moved to Aberdeen, Arbroath, and then Dundee in 1842 before finally moving to Linthouse in 1870. Up to 1871, the firm specialised in sailing vessels, but from this date they moved into building higher class cargo liners and passenger ships. They also built naval vessels for the two world wars.

Famous ships built by the company include the ill-fated liner *Tuscania* (1915), the fast minelayers *Manxman* (1941) and *Ariadne* (1943), aircraft carrier *Ocean* (1945) and RFA *Sir Galahad* (1966) which was lost in the Falklands in 1982.

As already mentioned, Fred Stephen and his son John were notable yachtsmen. Fred's other son Alexander Murray Stephen, who took control of the yard in 1932, had a technical interest in welding and under his influence the company pioneered the extensive use of this technology on the Clyde.

The shipbuilding assets and activities of Alexander Stephen & Sons Ltd were transferred to the short-lived Upper Clyde Shipbuilders (UCS) in 1968, although the engineering and ship repairing side of the business remained in family hands until 1976.

Florinda

The Yacht

In 1930, Lloyds Register of Yachts listed *Florinda* as a big ketch of 101 feet length overall (86.6 feet on the waterline) and 19.2 feet beam.

Florinda was originally built as yawl for a Mr William Jessop by Camper & Nicholson at Gosport in 1873. She had a long life and proved so unexpectedly speedy that she became known as the "Gosport Mistake".

Florinda began her impressive career by winning six 1st and five 2nd places in her first season. In 1877, she secured nine prizes worth £553 and did even better in 1878, with ten 1st and two 2nd places worth £736 to her credit, as well as winning the Nore to Dover race the same year. She then won eight 1st and six 2nd prizes in 1880, and won the Commodore's Cup in 1881.

FLORINDA as a Yawl
(PHOTO © BEKEN)

Florinda was altered in 1911 from a yawl (mizzen mast placed aft of the rudder post) to a ketch (mizzen mast placed forward of rudder post). She ended her years as the clubhouse for the Royal Motor Yacht Club in Poole in the 1930s.

Owner – James Pender

For a few years around 1900, *Florinda* was owned by Sir James Pender (1841-1921). He was a Director of several electrical and technology related companies including Telegraph Construction & Maintenance Company taken over decades later by British Insulated Callender's Cables (BICC), Globe Telegraph Trust, United States Cable Company Ltd and Eastman Kodak (USA). Pender served as Chairman of Eastman Kodak (UK) from 1898 until 1913. He also sat as Member of Parliament for Northamptonshire Mid from 1895 to 1900. In 1897 he was created a Baronet, of Thornby Hall in the County of Northampton.

In addition to *Florinda*, James Pender also owned other famous yachts including *Brynhild, Brynhild II, Lamorna* and *Siesta*.

In 1902 Pender won the King's Cup at the Royal Yacht Squadron Regatta at Cowes with *Brynhild*, beating *Meteor* the yacht of the German Emperor Kaiser Wilhelm II. On that occasion, the trophy was presented to him by Edward VII. In 1904 at Kiel in Germany, Kaiser Wilhelm had to present Pender and *Brynhild* with the prize for the Imperial Yacht Club Regatta. In the 1908 Cowes Regatta, Pender's yacht *Brynhild* defeated Sir Thomas Lipton's *Shamrock*.

Other Owners

Florinda had many owners after Pender. These included Sir John Edwards-Moss (1904 to 1910), KE Lee Guinness (1920), WC Bersey (1927, 1930) and Ernest R Barrow (1937).

Loch Broom Men

Alex MacNab from Loggie is reported to have worked on *Florinda*. The photograph depicts Duncan MacNab with two men from Harris.

Duncan MacNab (L) of FLORINDA, with Donald Morrison & John MacDonald (both from Harris) of PELAGIA
(Ullapool Museum)

Gleniffer

The Yacht

Gleniffer was a large and handsome three-masted steel schooner, designed by GL Watson and built by D&W Henderson at Meadowside, Glasgow (yard number 413) in 1899.

Her first owner was James Coats Junior of the Paisley thread-making family. After his death in 1912, she passed to a Noel Pemberton Billing of London and was renamed *Utopia*. She was named after the Gleniffer Braes which are a range of hills to the south of Paisley, on the boundary between Renfrewshire and North Ayrshire.

Gleniffer is by far the largest sailing vessel in this book. Her overall length was 185ft, with a length between perpendiculars of 157ft and beam of 26.7ft. Gross tonnage was 316 and Thames measurement was 496 tons. Originally built without an engine, she was often accompanied by the owner's steam yacht *Triton*, which acted as a tug on windless days.

GLENIFFER at Lamlash Bay, Isle of Arran, 1904, awaiting return of Scottish Antarctic Expedition
(permission of Cambridge University)

GLENIFFER (with 2 masts) in Laksevag near Bergen, Norway (GL WATSON)

The Owner – James Coats Junior

James Coats Junior (1841-1912), was the son of Thomas Coats (1809–1883) whose father James had founded the huge Coats thread-making empire of Paisley.

The story of the Coats firm is complicated, involving British as well as North American based branches, run by various members of the Coats family. It became closely involved with the neighbouring Paisley firm of Clark. The first James Coats took up weaving in 1802, and in 1826 opened a cotton mill at Ferguslie in Paisley to produce his own thread. His sons, James and Peter, took over in 1830 and founded the firm of J&P Coats in 1830. Their brother, Thomas (an engineer) joined the company, making an ideal combination with the shawl-making experience of James and Peter's training as an accountant.

The firm expanded rapidly, both in Scotland and internationally, particularly in the USA which was their largest market in the mid-19th century. In 1896 Clark and Coats agreed to work together but maintained separate names until 1952 when J&P Coats and the Clark Thread Co. fully merged their names and products. In the USA, the combination of Clark and Coats was regarded as a threat to the American thread companies, and in 1913 the US government filed a lawsuit against the Paisley firms for trade violations, notably price-fixing. This led in 1914 to the formal separation of the US based operations from those in Scotland.

By 1904 10,000 people were employed in the Paisley mills, but the 1980s saw the beginning of the end, and operations in Paisley ceased in the 1990s. Despite this, the modern incarnation of the Coats group remains a globally important manufacturer and distributor of sewing thread and supplies.

James Coats Junior never married and had no children. Towards the end of his life he seems to have become something of an eccentric recluse. In his younger years he was a keen yachtsman, serving as president of the Royal Clyde Yacht Club, and is known to have owned at least 16 yachts. The *Gleniffer* undertook at least two extended cruises to the Baltic in the early 20th century.

At Coats's death in 1912, he owned six yachts, ranging from the 3 ton cutter, *Sprite*, through *Brunette* to his famous 1883 racing cutter *Marjorie* (72 tons), her steam tender/tug *Iris* (68 tons), and the steam yacht *Triton* (337 tons, now *Madiz*) which was tender/tug to the 1899 schooner *Gleniffer* (496 tons). According to one obituary, none of this magnificent fleet had sailed for many years, but they were commissioned each spring with more than 70 crew always ready.

In his later years the *Gleniffer* was annually moved from her winter quarters at the James Watt Dock at Greenock, taken to her moorings in Gourock Bay, and remained there with her steam-powered companion *Triton* until the end of the season. It seemed that James Coats disliked the idea of depriving sixty or seventy men of their summer employment. When the state of his health finally made it obvious that he should never cruise again, he still maintained the yachts in the care of their officers, and kept in touch with all the discarded hands at Christmas, wherever they might be.

In 1884 James Coats commissioned the striking house of *Dunselma* above Strone Point which separates Loch Long and the Holy Loch on the Clyde. This "yachting lodge" is a striking expression of the conspicuous wealth of the late 19th century industrialists. When Coats died, it was said that he had not set foot in the house for years, and that he had probably never been in it more than twenty times since it was built, though it was always kept in a state of complete readiness for a visit. Following his death, *Dunselma* was sold to Walter Bergius (member of the family associated with Teacher's whisky and Kelvin diesel engines). In 1941, the villa passed to the Scottish Youth Hostel Association and served as a youth hostel until 1965.

The Coats family donated large sums of money to the town of Paisley and other worthy causes throughout Scotland. Thomas Coats best-known gifts to Paisley were the Observatory and the Fountain Gardens. Peter Coats provided a library to the town, whereupon Paisley became only the third place in Scotland to have a library and museum run by the local council.

Dunselma - former Coats "yachting lodge"
(cc-by-sa/2.0 - © Leslie Barrie - geograph.org.uk/p/3410293)

Children at Scoraig School, Little Loch Broom, c. 1910, with Coats schoolbags on display
(Ullapool Museum)

To encourage their education, James Coats Junior provided schoolbags for the school-children of north and west Scotland. He also arranged for the sending of 4000 libraries in double fronted bookcases to rural communities with no library of their own. He appeared to be doing for these communities what Carnegie had done for the towns and cities of Scotland. In Ullapool, the Coats library of 400 volumes was supplied in 1904 and placed in the Reading Room which had been established in 1897. By the 1960s, the village library had declined to a few surviving volumes held in a bookcase at the school.

James and his brother Andrew were the principal financiers of the Scottish National Antarctic Expedition (1902-1904) which used the research ship *Scotia*. They provided over £30,000 of the £36,000 total costs of this venture led by William Speirs Bruce which undertook a scientific exploration of the Weddell Sea. This expedition explored a 150 mile stretch of the Antarctic coast which was named as Coats Land.

On the expedition's return to Scotland in July 1904, the Coats yacht *Gleniffer* met the *Scotia* at Lamlash Bay in Arran. A formal reception was held at the Marine Biological Station, Millport, at which a telegram of congratulation from King Edward VII was read in front of 400 guests.

The Designer – GL Watson

George Lennox Watson (1851 – 1904) was a famous Scottish naval architect and yacht designer. He was born in Glasgow, son of Thomas Lennox Watson, a doctor at the Glasgow Royal Infirmary.

From the age of 16, Watson served as an apprentice draughtsman at the Glasgow shipyard of Robert Napier, and later at the J&A Inglis yard in Glasgow. In 1873, at the age of 22, he set up what was probably the world's first yacht design office.

He soon attracted design commissions from high-profile clients such as the Coats of Paisley, the Vanderbilt family, Earl Dunraven, Sir Thomas Lipton, the Rothschild family, and Kaiser Wilhelm II of Germany.

Watson designed four unsuccessful challengers for the America's Cup; the *Thistle* (1887) for the Scottish syndicate, *Valkyrie II* (1893) and *Valkyrie III* (1895) for Lord Dunraven, and *Shamrock II* (1901) for Sir Thomas Lipton. Probably his most famous sailing yacht design was the *Britannia* (1893) for Edward Prince of Wales (future King Edward VII), and later passed on to his son King George V. She had a long and successful racing career before being scuttled in 1936 after the death of George V.

Alfred Mylne (designer of *Vadura, Thendara* and others in this book) worked for GL Watson before setting up his own office in 1896.

VALKYRIE II (left) racing VIGILANT
in the 1893 America's Cup
(US Library of Congress)

The Watson firm also became famous for its steam yacht designs and work on lifeboats for the Royal National Lifeboat Institution (RNLI), with Watson becoming chief consulting Naval Architect to the RNLI in 1887. After Watson's early death at 54, the company was managed by former Chief Draughtsman James Rennie Barnett, who further developed the firm's reputation for luxury steam yachts. The Barnett and GL Watson company association with the RNLI continued into the late 1960s.

After effectively ceasing operations, the company was purchased by William Collier in 2001 and relocated from Scotland to Liverpool. The business is now connected with the design, restoration and replica builds of large yachts, supported by the original design archive which was temporarily housed in the Mitchell Library in Glasgow.

Loch Broom Men

Kenneth MacRae (an uncle of Allan "Mor" MacKenzie) served on the *Gleniffer*, journeying as far as the Baltic. He also worked on the *Zara*, owned by Peter Coats, cousin of James Junior. Willie MacKenzie, later Skipper of the *Roska*, also worked on the *Gleniffer* in his younger years.

Golden Eagle

The Yacht

Golden Eagle was a steam yacht built of steel by Ramage & Ferguson at Leith in 1899, to a design by GL Watson. She had dimensions of 159ft length overall and 25ft beam. These gave her tonnages of 356 gross and 455 Thames Measurement.

In 1909 she was sold to Mr Arthur Bowley of Harlow, Essex in 1909 and renamed *Vanessa*. During this period she was commanded by Captain L Cockrell of Wivenhoe, had a Wivenhoe crew, and was regularly laid up at Wivenhoe on the River Colne.

Vanessa was loaned to the government for naval work in October 1914 and her entire crew volunteered to sail with her. She was fitted out at Portsmouth with protective iron plating and served as an auxiliary patrol yacht, mounting two 6 pounder guns. Some of her patrol duties were carried out in the Minch, where she was a frequent caller at places such as Aultbea and Ullapool. Captain Cockrell's log of these patrols is preserved at Wivenhoe and extracts are available online. In February 1917 she became *Vanessa II* so that her name could be given to a new destroyer. She was returned to her owner in March 1919.

The yacht was owned from 1925 to 1934 by ship owner William Raeburn of Helensburgh and renamed *Golden Eagle*. During the Second World War she again served on naval duty as the *Carina*.

GOLDEN EAGLE
(GL WATSON)

Above: GOLDEN EAGLE as VANESSA
in the River Colne before WW1
(image reproduced by permission of Nottage
Maritime Institute, Essex)

Left: **Loch Broom Men** Crew of the
GOLDEN EAGLE (Roderick "Nelson"
MacKenzie on right) with guest
(Eric MacKenzie photo)

The Owner

Sir William Hannay Raeburn (1850 – 1934) was a Scottish ship owner and Unionist Party politician who served as a Member of Parliament between 1918 and 1923.

In 1873 Raeburn co-founded a shipping company called Raeburn & Dunn, subsequently re-named Raeburn & Verel. By 1900 the company operated around 12 steamers, serving ports in Europe, America and the Far East. In 1902 Raeburn & Verel formed the Monarch Steamship Company Ltd.

William Raeburn played an important part in connection with most of the shipping legislation of the time, notably the Merchant Shipping Act and the Workmen's Compensation Act of 1906. For many years he was Chairman of the Clyde Navigation Trust. In 1916 Raeburn was appointed president of the UK Chamber of Shipping and on his retirement from that position that he was awarded a knighthood for services to shipping.

Raeburn was born in Glasgow, but moved to Helensburgh towards the end of the 19th century where he lived in *Woodend*, a splendid mansion in Millig Street. After his death this served for a time as a St Bride's School boarding house. Today the property is converted into flats and has modern homes built in its extensive grounds.

Hotspur

The Yacht

Hotspur was built as a wooden yawl at Cowes in 1874. She was 76.5ft long, 18.1ft beam and 102 tons Thames measurement (48 gross tons).

From 1903 to 1907 she was owned by John Workman of Northern Ireland, although her port continued to be stated as Glasgow. The initials of the Royal Northern Ireland Yacht Club are displayed on the Loch Broom crew jerseys (see later entries for Munro family).

Amazingly, the yacht has survived into the 21st century, although not in sailing condition. In 1998, *Hotspur* was featured in a home and interior design magazine, having been saved and used as a houseboat at West Mersea, Essex since 1914 [17]. Her survival is no doubt due to the longevity of her original 2½ inch thick old-growth teak planking, and the attraction of her beautiful interior furniture. The yacht is available as a holiday let, advertised on the internet.

Left: Saloon of the HOTSPUR (as houseboat, 1998) showing maple panels with teak surrounds
(from *25 Beautiful Homes* magazine, October 1998)

Right: HOTSPUR in Essex, 1998
(*Beautiful Homes* magazine, October 1998)

The Owner

John Workman was a member of a prominent family of Belfast industrialists, involved in the linen and muslin manufacturing business.

Another family member, Frank Workman, founded the Workman Clark shipbuilding business in Belfast in 1880, together with George Clark who was the second son of Paisley thread manufacturer James Clark (mentioned elsewhere in this book). The firm was connected by marriage to the Smith family who owned the City Line of Glasgow and also to the Allan shipping family (also yacht owners).

Hotspur passed through multiple owners both before and after the Workman period.

Loch Broom Men

William Munro from Rhiroy worked on the *Hotspur*. His photograph (in a *Hotspur* jersey) is reproduced in the following chapter. The Workman family later owned the *Morna* on which William Munro was also employed.

Jeano (ex Tritonia)

The Yacht – History in UK

Jeano was a top racing yacht of the 15-Metre class, originally named *Tritonia*, and built in 1910 for Graham C Lomer, of London.

After William Fife's *Shimna* (1907), *Tritonia* was the second 15-Metre racing yacht built by Alexander Robertson & Sons Ltd, Sandbank. Her design was created in 1909 by the famous Scottish naval architect Alfred Mylne (Design No. 177), who was by then regularly competing with William Fife III for the season's fastest new yacht.

She was a 51 ton racing cutter of 75 feet deck length, laid down as Boat No. 67 at the Robertson yard. By 13th January 1910 construction was underway - the keel, stem and sternpost were in position and the lead keel had been laid. By 3rd February the *Yachtsman* magazine reported that the framing was in place and the yacht had been officially named *Tritonia*.

After a very rushed preparation, *Tritonia* made a poor start to the new racing season in the south. At the Royal Thames Yacht Club in May 1910, the new Mylne designed yacht was the centre of attention, but it was reported, *"she made such a poor start that nothing but a fluke could save her".* However, she achieved several wins later in the season.

The Field reported 60 starts for the 15-Metre class in 1910; of which 22 (36%) were in light wind conditions, 13 (22%) "moderate", 18 (30%) "fresh" and seven (12%) "strong"; a fairly typical summer for racing.

A change of ownership and name occurred in 1911 when Sir John Hume Campbell of Greenlaw, Berwick-shire, bought *Tritonia* and renamed her as *Jeano*. She won the 15-Metre race at Felixstowe in September 1911, with her new sail number D-3.

Conditions in 1911 were apparently more benign; 34 out of 56 starts (61%) were "light", ten "moderate" (18%), nine "fresh" (16%) and just three "strong" (5%). In contrast, strong winds caused many cancellations in the 1912 season and only about 43 starts occurred out of 60 planned. Of those, conditions for 12 (27%) were "light", nine (19%) "moderate", 11 (25%) "fresh" and 11 (23%) "strong" or even "gale".

Jeano was bought by W R Reid of Edinburgh in 1913 and converted from a cutter to a yawl in 1916. Both Hume Campbell and Reid would likely have belonged to the Royal Forth Yacht Club, which probably explains the RFYC on the jerseys of the Loch Broom men.

The painting by Bill Bishop depicts yachts of the 15-Metre Class, short tacking against the tide, racing in the Solent before 1914. The *Lady Anne* (D10) is in the lead, *Hispania* (D5, number hidden) and *Jeano* (D3) come next. They are closely followed by *Mariska*, (D1, just tacking), and *Sophie Elizabeth* (D6).

Sale out of Scotland

David Hutchinson has researched the history of the *Jeano* and other Robertson built vessels [15]. In 1918 *Jeano* was acquired by Thor Thorenson Jnr and taken to Norway, with a new set of Ratsey & Lapthorn sails. She was to go through many Scandinavian owners.

Einar W Egeberg of Christiana (now Oslo), Norway, purchased her in 1921. S Kloumann acquired *Jeano* in 1929 and she remained based in Oslo although Kloumann was a director of Aktieselskap Norsk Aeroplanfabrikk (the Norwegian Aircraft Factory Ltd) at Tønsberg in southern Norway. Kloumann had previously commissioned the last 15-Metre ever built; the Johan Anker designed *Neptune* of 1917.

Jeano was sold to Olav Ringdal of the Olav Ringdal Shipping Company in 1947 and for a while named *Gerd II*, after his daughter. A Kermath 6-cylinder petrol motor was installed in 1947 and she was altered from a yawl to an auxiliary Bermudan cutter in 1948. In 1954 Ringdal renamed *Gerd II* as *Rinola*, a derivation of his own name (**Rin**gdal, **Ol**av). The last record of the *Rinola* in 'Lloyd's Register of Yachts' is in 1956 when she was still owned by Olav Ringdal and based in Oslo.

Ringdal sold the yacht in the late 1950s to his friend Adolf Westphal, the head of the shipyard in Kiel, Germany – Kieler Howaldt Werke (later merged with the Deutsche Werft yard in Hamburg and known as H-D-W). Westphal (or King Adolf as he was known) renamed the yacht *Fortuna II*.

15-Metre yacht JEANO
as Tritonia 1910
(PHOTO © BEKEN)

Inset: *15 metres off Cowes before 1914*
featuring JEANO D3
(painting by Bill Bishop)

Brazilian Navy Training Vessel

Fortuna II was presented to the Brazilian Navy as a gift in the 1970s, when Brazil purchased submarines from H-D-W/Ferrostaal. The yacht was in poor shape and was taken to Brazil as deck cargo by the *Lloyd Rotterdam* in 1978. She was renamed *Cisne Branco* (White Swan) and became the first of three Brazilian Navy sail training vessels to bear this name. After extensive repairs she undertook an 8-month voyage across the Atlantic and back to Brazil in 1980.

After acquisition of a new *Cisne Branco*, the boat was renamed *Albatroz* in 1981. Her present whereabouts and status are uncertain, although there are reports of a possible sighting at a small naval harbour in Rio de Janeiro in 2015.

CISNE BRANCO (ex JEANO)
returning to Guanabara Bay, Brazil in
1980 after her Atlantic cruise

The Builder - Robertson's Yard, Sandbank

Alexander Robertson (born in Inverkip on 29 August 1851), was the son of a fisherman from Tarskavaig on the Isle of Skye. His parents moved to Sandbank on the north side of the Firth of Clyde in 1859 to run the village Post Office.

Alexander Robertson served his apprenticeship as a boat builder in Dunoon and Govan, and then started repairing boats in a small workshop at Sandbank in 1876. His yard went on to become one of the foremost wooden boat builders in Scotland and was highly regarded for the quality of its workmanship.

By 1900 he had most of the infrastructure required to produce high class wooden boats in place: sawmills, workshops, building-sheds, pier, slipway, stores, paint shop, engine house, sail loft and workers' houses.

The peak years of Robertson's yard were in the early 1900s when they began building 12 and 15 Metre racing yachts. Robertson's was chosen to build the first 15-Metre yacht designed by the legendary William Fife III (*Shimna*, 1907). He also constructed the 15-Metre *Tritonia* (1910), later named *Jeano* – designed by Alfred Mylne. Alexander Robertson died in 1937.

Loch Broom Men

This photograph of *Jeano* crewmen Allan MacKenzie (Allan Mor) and Kenny "Buie" MacKenzie, both from Letters, was taken at Gourock in 1913.

Kentra

The Yacht

Kentra was built in 1923 by William Fife (yard number 707) as a cruising ketch for Kenneth Clark. She was named after a bay on the coast of the owner's Ardnamurchan estate.

Allan "Mor" MacKenzie (L) and
Kenneth "Buie" MacKenzie (R),
(Ullapool Museum)

Kentra is 82ft long with 17.6ft beam and a Thames measurement of 87 tons. Her hull is planked in teak above the waterline and copper-sheathed pine below, laid over oak and iroko frames. *Kentra* was originally built with a bowsprit and gaff rig, but after the death of third owner Barclay Hogarth in 1951 she was converted to a Bermudan stemhead cutter (single-masted) rig. During her 1990s restoration, the original two-masted gaff rig was reinstated.

The history of engines installed in *Kentra* is interesting, showing the move from paraffin to diesel and the increase in power over the years. She was originally built with a 30hp Bergius paraffin motor, which was replaced by a 45hp Gardner diesel in 1951. In 1963 this was exchanged for a 180hp Caterpillar engine which lasted for about forty years before it was replaced by a 140hp Yanmar

After various adventures in the Mediterranean and around the world, *Kentra* was bought unseen at a Sheriff's auction in Helensburgh in 1993 and restored at Fairlie Restorations on the Hamble. She undertook a leisurely circumnavigation from 1999 to 2003 via the Panama Canal, New Zealand and the Suez Canal. *Kentra* was then laid up for seven years at Fairlie in a shed near

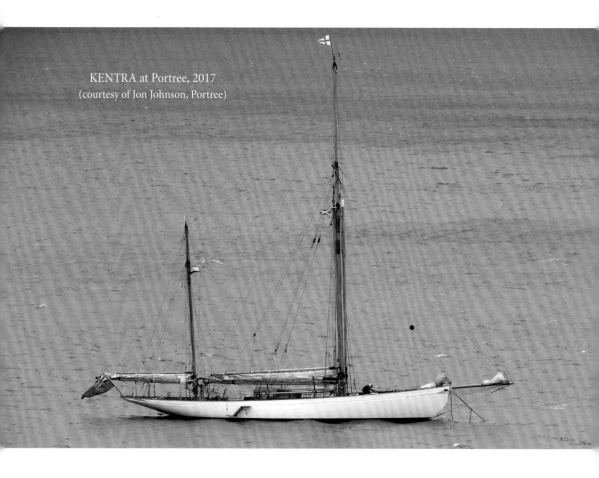

KENTRA at Portree, 2017
(courtesy of Jon Johnson, Portree)

the place where she was built. In the winter of 2012-13 she was re-commissioned for the fourth Fife Regatta on the Clyde. At that time she was advertised for sale with an asking price of £2.45 million, but for now *Kentra* may regularly be seen cruising the West Coast of Scotland, as she did ninety years ago.

Owners

Kentra's first owner Kenneth Clark (1868–1932) was a member of the Paisley thread-making dynasty, described in the chapter on *Vadura*. Clark was notorious for ordering expensive yachts and keeping them for only a short time. In the case of *Kentra*, he kept her for just one season before selling her in 1924 to Charles Livingstone (1857 - 1937) of Birkenhead whose family were among the early investors in the Cunard shipping line. From 1936 to 1951, *Kentra* was owned by Barclay Hogarth (1878 - 1951) of the Hogarth shipping family.

This company was founded in 1868 by Hugh Hogarth (1840 - 1904) of Ardrossan. His sons were Samuel Crawford Hogarth (1874-1950), Hugh Hogarth Jr. (1876-1954) and Barclay

Hogarth. In 1881 the company ordered their first steamship and when Hugh died Samuel gradually disposed of the sailing vessels and built up the fleet of steamers. By 1914 the company owned 23 ships, but 14 were lost during World War One. The fleet was rebuilt and by 1939 was one of the largest privately owned shipping companies in the world. During the Second World War 20 of the 39 ships were lost, and another rebuilding effort was required in the post-war years.

Samuel Crawford Hogarth died in 1950 and the management of the company was taken over by other family members. Another Hugh Hogarth (b. 1909, son of Samuel Crawford Hogarth) served as Chairman and died in 1973. The company had moved into the bulk carrier trade in 1965 and in 1968 joined with Lyle Shipping Co. to form Scottish Ship Management Ltd. In 1986 that company ceased trading.

The Hogarth shipping business was also known as the Baron Line, and nicknamed "*Hungry Hogarths*", due to its reputation for being overly economical, especially with the food for the crew. Two of the politer verses from a song "celebrating" this reputation are reproduced below.

Ye may have sailed in sailing ships,
ye may have sailed in tramps,
Ye may have been in whalers off the
Grand Newfoundland Banks,
Ye may have been in tanker ships,
and had a bloody rough time,
But ye've never been through the mill
'til ye've sailed with the Baron Line !

The cook he was from Senegal,
the steward from Tiree
We had mutton for the dinner,
and curry for the tea
The mates they got the bacon,
the crew we got the rind
You've never seen starvation lads
'till you sailed with the Baron Line

Owners after Hogarth

After Barclay Hogarth died, *Kentra* passed to Charles Brassey Thorne. He converted her to a stem-head Bermudan ketch and took her to the Mediterranean. During this period she hosted many glamorous guests, including Brigitte Bardot and Errol Flynn.

She then passed through several more hands, before eventually returning to the UK where she lay unused for many years. *Kentra* was bought by Swiss-German businessman Ernst Klaus in the early 1990s and it was he who he commissioned Fairlie Restorations in 1993 to undertake her major rebuild.

Loch Broom Men

William "Jock" MacKenzie was on *Kentra* after World War Two. He worked on her for one season before going deep sea sailing with the Baron Line (the Hogarth company).

Lulworth (ex Terpsichore)

The Yacht

Lulworth is a large gaff cutter built of composite wooden planking on steel frames in 1920 in only eight months by the White Brothers Yard, Southampton. She was designed by Herbert White as a racing cruiser rather than a pure racing yacht. Consequently, she had a high freeboard, 2 feet high bulwarks, and a luxurious interior, later documented by the Victoria & Albert Museum.

Today she is the largest gaff cutter afloat, with a length on deck of 122 feet and a mast as high as a 17-story building (171 feet). *Lulworth* has never been regarded as a great beauty, having an appearance conveying power rather than grace. However, she is the only Big Boat from the 1920s era left in her as-built state and is the sole survivor of the famous Big Five. As a result, she is well documented, and there are many sources of information regarding her history [3,4].

Richard H Lee from Torbay originally ordered the yacht (then named *Terpsichore)* to provide competition for the King's *Britannia*. After four years he sold her to Herbert Weld who gave her the name *Lulworth* and made some crucial changes during his brief ownership. She had two more owners during her short racing career between 1920 and 1930.

She was an extreme design and suffered various teething problems with her rigging and deck equipment in her early years. Because of post-war shortages of prime spruce, the lower part of the mast was originally made of steel instead of wood and this handicapped *Terpsichore*. Overall, she underperformed compared to older Big Class racers like the royal yacht *Britannia I* (1893), Sir Thomas Lipton's Fife designed 23-Metre *Shamrock* (1908), and the Herreshoff designed schooner *Westward* (1910).

During her debut 1920 season *Terpsichore* made only six starts and was soon withdrawn to have her rig adjusted. This work was carried out in Gosport by Camper & Nicholson who evaluated the rig and drafted an alternative. Although the issues were not resolved then, the relationship with designer Charles E Nicholson continued until he finally solved her problems in 1924 by redesigning the rig with a wooden lower mast and adjusting the keel balance.

Change of Name and Success

In 1924, Lee sold *Terpsichore* to Herbert Weld, owner of the Lulworth estate and castle in Dorset. At the age of 72, Mr Weld was following in the footsteps of his grandfather Joseph Weld, a founder member of the Royal Yacht Squadron, who had owned two yachts called *Lulworth*. It was at this point that the name change from *Terpsichore* to *Lulworth* was made. Her paint scheme was also changed from dark to white.

After Charles Nicholson had made the final alterations that brought out her latent capacity, the yacht won 10 times from 16 starts during the 1924 season. In 1925, *Lulworth* competed in 28 races and was placed first, second or third in all of them, achieving nine first, eleven second and eight third places against *Shamrock, White Heather II, Westward* and *Britannia*.

Sir Mortimer Singer & Archie Hogarth – 1926 to 1930

The successes of 1925 attracted the attention of one of the famous adventurers of the early 20th century, Sir Mortimer Singer (1863-1929). Mortimer was an Anglo-American son of Isaac Singer the sewing machine millionaire, well known for his flying and motoring exploits. He could easily afford to make Herbert Weld an irresistible offer to take over *Lulworth*.

The 1926 season was another successful one for *Lulworth* and the second year at the top of her class. The achievement of 13 first places was a record performance among the Big Five. Although *Shamrock* managed to win 13 races two years later, she competed in three more events (32 as opposed to *Lulworth*'s 29 in 1926).

Sir Mortimer Singer commissioned the new Bermudan rigged racing yacht *Astra* in 1928, but one year later he took a barbiturate overdose and died. A verdict of suicide was returned.

AA Paton, member of a family firm of Liverpool cotton traders, was listed by Lloyds Register as the owner from 1928 until 1935 when his executors disposed of the vessel.

The last two years of *Lulworth*'s racing career were under the ownership of Paton and captaincy of Archie Hogarth of Port Bannatyne, Bute, famous for his wins with the cutter *Cambria*. Hogarth first became a Skipper onboard the cutter *Calluna* in 1893 and then helmed many top yachts from *Shamrock I* to *Cambria*. In 1929 Hogarth skippered *Lulworth* to 19 wins from 40 starts. Alec (Lally) MacKenzie from Lochbroom was on *Lulworth* in 1929.

Hogarth liked Essex men in his crew – and did not limit himself only to Scots. In 1926 *Lulworth* had a mixed team of 26 – from the Clyde, Essex, the Solent and the West Country. Many men were happy to leave the *Lulworth* – her gear was too heavy for a crew of 26 and dangerous as well. For example, she broke her mast in 1926 off the Isle of Wight. Some earlier gaff cutters had been larger, but they had crews of 30 to 35.

The 1930 season was also very successful for *Lulworth*, with the handicapping rules being more suitable for her. Out of 45 starts, she won 22, despite having to compete against the largest Big Class fleet ever assembled off the British coast. The competitors included *Britannia, White Heather II, Westward, Astra, Cambria, Candida* and *Shamrock V*. This *Shamrock* was Sir Thomas Lipton's last challenger for the America's Cup, and the first J-Class yacht to be built in the UK.

The fifteenth America's Cup contest of 1930 featured the Bermudan rigged J-Class designs which made all gaff-rigged racers obsolete. Despite *Lulworth*'s early successes against the

LULWORTH at speed upwind
(PHOTO © BEKEN)

Inset: Deck of LULWORTH
(one of Lally's photographs)
(Ullapool Museum)

J-Class *Shamrock V* (1930) before the America's Cup, the era of the Big Class came to an end and *Lulworth*'s racing career was terminated.

A fatal accident in 1930 probably confirmed Paton's decision to retire from the racing scene rather than convert *Lulworth* to a Bermudan rig to compete under the new rules. *Lulworth*, with Hogarth at the helm, was involved in a collision with the 12-Metre *Lucilla*. This was caused by *Lucilla* tacking close under her bow and *Lulworth*, running before the wind with all sails set, being unable to avoid the situation in time. William Saunders, steward on *Lucilla,* was trapped below decks and drowned.

Later History - 1930s to 1980s

In the economic depression of the 1930s, no other buyer was prepared to invest the large sums involved in converting *Lulworth* to Bermudan rig and the J-Class rules. Instead, she was converted into a cruising ketch by May Beazley who briefly owned her in the middle of the decade.

After owning her for less than two years, Mrs Beazley sold *Lulworth* to the chocolate magnate Carl Bendix. Her first engine was installed and the new owners made plans for a round-the-world voyage. The imminent start of the Second World War forced a more mundane destination on *Lulworth* - a mud berth close to the Camper & Nicholson yard.

A further change of ownership occurred in 1943, although Norman Hartly bought and sold *Lulworth* without ever seeing her in the water. During a German bombing raid on the English south coast, the yacht's main mast was struck by debris from a nearby hit. The mast fell against the mizzen which, in turn, collapsed onto the stern and smashed the taffrail.

Most boats would have been 'decommissioned' at this point, but *Lulworth* was saved by Richard and Irene Lucas who, in July 1947, saw her lying in a neglected state. They decided to pay around £3,000 for *Lulworth*, which at the time was a lot of money for a boat requiring so much work.

Lulworth was brought back to the White Brothers yard for a partial restoration. As the plan was for her to serve as a well-furnished floating holiday retreat, there was no intention to restore her sailing capability. For the first few years she was used as a weekend home, moored off the *Jolly Sailor* pub on the River Hamble. In 1955 Richard and Irene moved permanently onboard and shifted to a mud berth further up the Hamble at Crableck Marina. After Richard Lucas died in 1968, his wife remained aboard, but *Lulworth* gradually fell into disrepair. Mrs Lucas was approached on various occasions to sell, and finally agreed to do so in the late 1980s.

Restoration

In January 1990 *Lulworth* was liberated from her mud berth and towed to Camper & Nicholson's yard in Gosport. She was bought by the Columbo-Vink family who transported her to Italy in the spring of 1990. However, this attempted restoration failed due to legal problems.

In 2001, *Lulworth* was rediscovered sitting outside at the Beconcini yard in La Spezia, Italy by Dutch entrepreneur Johan van den Bruele and project manager Giuseppe Longo. A sale was agreed and *Lulworth* was transported to the Classic Yacht Darsena yard in nearby Viareggio.

There, *Lulworth* was brought back to life in a multi-million-euro restoration that lasted five years. This restoration used traditional methods and returned the yacht as closely as possible to her original state, saving 70% of her furnishings and 80% of her steel frames. The sail plan from 1926 was used to recreate *Lulworth*'s rig, which featured the world's tallest wooden mast.

Rebuilt to Lloyd's Classification, she was relaunched in 2006 and immediately entered racing competition. *Lulworth* participates in classic and superyacht regattas in the Mediterranean.

Lulworth – Technical Details

Dimension		Sail	
Length over spars	46.30m (152ft)	Total	1,450 m² (15,600 ft²)
Length on deck	37.2m (122ft)	Upwind sails only	828 m²
Length waterline	24.60m (80.7ft)	Main sail	465 m² (5,000 ft²)
Beam	7.60m (24.9ft)	Topsail	133 m²
Draught	5.20m (17ft)	Staysail	114 m²
Displacement	180 tonnes	Jib	69.5 m²
Mast height	52.0m (170.6ft)	Jib Topsail	46.5 m²
Boom length	27.6m (90.6ft)	Spinnaker	500 m²

Loch Broom Men

The photographs below show Lally (Alec MacKenzie) on *Lulworth*.

Left: Alec "Lally" MacKenzie (back left) at sea in LULWORTH, 1929 (Alec "Lally" MacKenzie photo, Ullapool Museum)

Right: Alec "Lally" MacKenzie (back centre) on LULWORTH at Camper & Nicholson's yard, 1929 (Alec "Lally" MacKenzie photo, Ullapool Museum)

Mafalda

The Yacht

Mafalda was a relatively small yacht (41ft length, 10ft beam and 8'6" ft draft), built in 1891 in London. She was owned on the south coast of England until the late 1920s. During the 1930s *Mafalda* had a succession of owners based in the Glasgow area, including a Mr McRoberts and an Alan MacKean. There is no record of her in the 1937 Lloyds Register of Yachts.

The Sailmaker – MacKenzie of Greenock

Despite being a rather humble vessel, the *Mafalda* shared her sailmaker with more glamorous sisters like *Fiumara* (1934), the Fife built *Satellite* and the *Vadura* (1926). The Clyde yachtsmen seemed to give a lot of their business to Greenock based sailmaker John MacKenzie, rather than the more famous English sailmakers such as Ratsey & Lapthorn. This business went into voluntary liquidation in 1951.

A son of this family was John Mackenzie (1876 –1949), who competed with the Royal Clyde Yacht Club at the 1908 Olympics. He was a crew member of the Scottish boat *Hera*, which won the gold medal in the 12-Metre class.

Mariella

The Yacht

Mariella is an unusual combination of an Alfred Mylne design (design number 390) and a William Fife build (yard number 824). She is one of only three yachts built at the Fife yard which were not designed by Fife. Completed in 1938, she displays modern features compared to most of the other yachts in this book, including a Bermudan rig and no bowsprit.

Mariella is a yawl with a mainsail of 1,480 ft^2 area and a mizzen of 278 ft^2. Her length is 79ft with a beam of 16.5ft, giving a Thames measurement of 74 tons.

Apparently, her build was initially quoted at £11,275 which was felt by Mylne to be expensive [6]. This cost equates to £152 per Thames ton, which can be compared with the rates of £133 and £125 per ton derived from the invoiced costs of the similar sized *Fiumara* (77 tons, 1934) and larger *Thendara* (147 tons, 1937), built at Stephens. Final labour costs at the Fife yard were £4,358 [6].

The Owner – Ronald Teacher

Mariella was commissioned by James D. Patterson, a wealthy Glasgow merchant, whose family

MARIELLA competing in the 2004 Antigua Classic Regatta
(Alamy)

had created Camp Coffee in Charlotte Street, Glasgow in 1876. Camp Coffee is a concentrated coffee-flavoured syrup, originally produced for soldiers serving in India as the basis for a drink that did not need grinding or brewing and could be served quickly in the field.

After only one season Patterson sold *Mariella* to Ronald McNairn Teacher (1900 - 1976) of the Teacher whisky distilling family. Teacher owned the yacht for most of her time in Scotland but had to wait until after World War Two to enjoy sailing her because the Royal Navy requisitioned *Mariella* in 1939. At the end of the war (in which he served at sea as a Lieutenant Commander) Ronald Teacher refitted the yacht and used her for the next 32 years cruising and racing.

Teacher was a keen sailor and Commodore of the Royal Clyde Yacht Club from 1938 to 1970. His house was *Aldonaig* at Rhu near Helensburgh.

In 1972 *Mariella* was sold and left the Clyde for the Mediterranean, where she went through several changes of ownership. Since then the yacht has been extensively refitted. Carlo Falcone bought her in 1992 and she has been based in Antigua for many years. *Mariella* regularly crosses oceans and can be seen sailing in many Classic Yacht Regattas around the world.

Loch Broom Men

Alec "Skene" MacKenzie, son of Kenny, worked on *Mariella* after World War Two.

Medea

The Yacht

This steam yacht was built in 1904 by Stephens of Linthouse for William MacAlister Hall of Torrisdale Castle near Carradale on the Mull of Kintyre. In May 1904 he decided his shooting season would be improved if the guests could be transported by yacht. Consequently, *Medea* was constructed in a record time of 51 days and was ready for the August shooting season. She was actually launched with steam up in her boiler. Murdo MacLean of Ullapool (married to Jane MacIver from Scoraig) was foreman during her construction.

In his declining years MacAlister Hall was said to use the *Medea* to voyage the short distance down the Kintyre coast to visit his barber in Campbeltown. She was (and is) 134ft long, 110ft waterline length and 16.65ft beam with 137 tons Thames measurement.

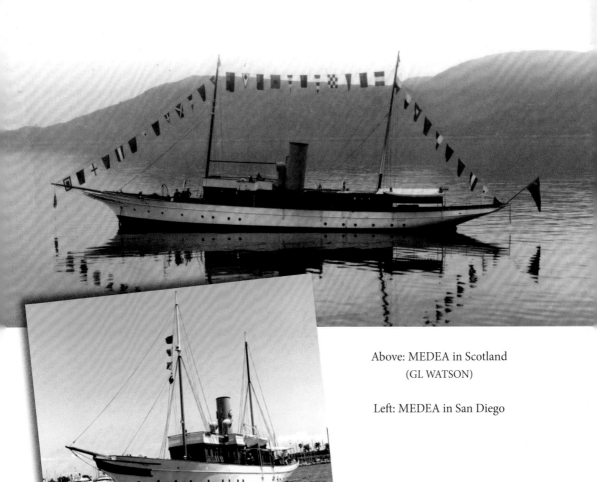

Above: MEDEA in Scotland
(GL WATSON)

Left: MEDEA in San Diego

In 1914 *Medea* was bought back by her builder John Stephen, and when he died in 1917, she was sold and later taken over by the French Navy and converted to a gunboat named *Corneille*. After the war, she returned to the UK as a yacht and resumed her old name.

Medea was bought again in 1930 by Frederic J. Stephen who had designed her and supervised her construction. When Fred died in 1934 she was sold once again. Early in World War II, *Medea* was taken over by the Royal Navy for use as a barrage balloon vessel in the approaches to the River Thames. Later she returned to Scotland and was used as an accommodation ship for Norwegian commando officers at Peterhead.

By 1946 *Medea* was a yacht again and passed through several owners until oilman Paul Whittier purchased her in 1971. He restored and donated *Medea* to the Maritime Museum of San Diego, where she arrived in 1973 and is still well preserved to this day.

Molin

The Yacht

Molin was a small yacht (the smallest in this book) built at Falmouth by RS Burt in 1930. She was 33ft long and 10.4ft beam with 13 tons Thames measurement, rigged as a Bermudan cutter and originally built with a petrol engine.

She seems to have been a yacht version of the local Falmouth Quay Punt working boat. Since the early part of the 19th century, the transom sterned Falmouth quay punts had serviced visiting ships: transporting supplies, messages, and crew to and from the town, as well as offering pilotage. In the days of sail and before the advent of radio, many sailing vessels arriving in the English Channel made for *"Falmouth for orders"* to receive instructions as to the final destination of their cargoes. To secure the business, the quay punts would race each other out to the ships in all weathers to be the first to offer their services.

By the early 20th century, with fewer ships calling at Falmouth and motor launches taking over, the days of the working punts were numbered. But their characteristics – seaworthy, suitable for short-handed sailing, relatively fast, and with roomy hulls – were also highly desirable for leisure cruising, and so not only were retired working boats converted to fulfil that role, but new examples were commissioned to be built as yachts. They were generally built with better materials than the working boats, and sometimes dispensed with the transom mounted mizzen mast of the original punts.

The Builder

The Burt family was one of three firms which specialised in building Falmouth Quay Punts, and is known to have built a total of 61 between the late 1870s and 1934 when RS Burt died.

Richard Stevens Burt served an apprenticeship with his father Charles, completing it in 1891. He later took over the family business, which was based on the Bar in Falmouth until 1926 when the expansion of Falmouth Docks forced a move to Flushing.

Owners

Molin seems to have been owned on the south coast of England and in the Channel Islands up until the 1950s. In 1953 *Molin* made a cruise in West Highland and Hebridean waters, as evidenced by a note on the back of the below photograph sent by Ronald Oliver to crewman Roderick MacKenzie.

Loch Broom Men

Roderick "Nelson" MacKenzie worked on this vessel after World War Two.

Roderick "Nelson" MacKenzie at the helm of MOLIN, 1953
(Eric MacKenzie photo)

Morna

The Yacht

Morna is a modestly sized wooden ketch, built in 1920 by Dickie of Tarbert, Loch Fyne. Peter Dickie designed the vessel with a canoe stern similar to those employed by Albert Strange.

Above: MORNA when crewed by William Munro
(courtesy Kenneth Munro)

Right: MORNA off Carrickfergus
in Belfast Lough, 21st Century

Morna has a length on deck 48 ft 6" and a beam of 11 ft 6" giving a Thames measurement of 22 tons. She is still in existence today.

Original Owners

Morna was built to the order of Captain Ronald Sillars (also featured in this book as the one-time owner of *Oceana*) who kept her briefly in Scotland until 1921. She was sold again in 1924 and owned in Northern Ireland for many years by Robert Workman, involved in linen manufacturing and the Workman Clark shipyard in Belfast.

Major Robert Workman (1879 - 1949) was the son of Thomas Workman (1843 - 1900). Thomas Workman was initially engaged in the family linen business and then shipbuilding, but was more famous for his interest in natural history, especially exotic spiders. His business travels took him to many countries where he was able to study the local natural history.

Thomas was an elder brother of Frank (1856 - 1927), founder of the Workman Clark shipyard, of which Thomas was a co-founder and vice-chairman. This so-called "Wee Yard" was formed in 1880 by Frank Workman and George Clark (1861 - 1935) who had both previously worked for the neighbouring Harland & Wolff (the "big yard"). Both partners also had good family connections to other ship owning and shipyard companies.

Workman Clark had a short history but was responsible for some notable performances, including the *Victorian* of 1904 for the Allan Line which was the first turbine driven transatlantic passenger liner. In World War One the yard employed 12,000 people and was an important producer and repairer of both merchant and naval ships. During the 1920s the structure of the yard ownership and its sister companies changed in a complicated fashion, reported to have been orchestrated by Robert Workman.

A reasonable output of ships continued until the Great Depression, but in 1935 the company went into receivership. The North yard was purchased by National Shipbuilders Security and dismantled, while Harland & Wolff reactivated the South Yard during World War Two.

Major Robert Workman served in the Royal Irish Rifles in World War One and was wounded at Ypres. During the 1920s he was an active climber in the Alps, as well as a keen yachtsman. Workman lived in the large mansion of *Craigdarragh* at Helen's Bay, County Down which he inherited from his father. After he died in 1949 the house was converted into a nursing home for the elderly.

Subsequent History

After Major Workman's death, *Morna* had several owners, including a GKW Pilkington when she was still recorded as being based at Glasgow.

In 1967 Stanley Reeves bought *Morna* and used her as a charter boat on the west coast of Scotland. He eventually sailed her single handed to the West Indies. She then found her way to Greece and Yugoslavia. John Pinkerton found the yacht in Croatia and transported her back to the UK in 1998 where he began a restoration, He had to sell her in 2002 because of failing health, and at that point *Morna* returned to Northern Ireland when she was purchased by Stephen Clarkson. Bangor, County Down was her base for 16 years until another sale in mid-2018.

Loch Broom Men

Morna required only a small crew, and when with the Workmans in the 1930s the professional hands consisted of only two persons, one of whom took on the cook/steward duties in addition to his other tasks.

The Munro family of Rhiroy were employed by the Workmans on the *Morna*, as they had been on the older *Hotspur*. A photograph of William Munro is included in the following chapter. By 1935 it seems that the *Morna* crewmen were from Tarskavaig in Skye rather than Loch Broom.

Narcissus

The Yacht

The *Narcissus* was a large steam yacht built by Fairfield Engineering Ltd, Govan, Glasgow as Yard No 437, launched on December 21st 1904. Her length was 254ft overall and 222.7ft waterline, with a beam of 27.7ft, giving a Thames tonnage of 816 (the largest in this book).

Unusually, she was powered by steam turbines, giving a speed of 14 knots. This was a very early application of this new technology on a leisure craft, considering that Charles Parson's famous demonstration with the *Turbinia* at Spithead only took place in 1897.

The first turbine passenger ship was the Clyde steamer *King Edward* of 1901, but the 1904 *Narcissus* was ahead of the first turbine battleship *HMS Dreadnought* (1906) and the large transatlantic liners *Mauretania* and *Lusitania* (1907).

History

The first owner of *Narcissus* was Alfred Edward Miller Mundy (1849 - 1920) who was the last squire of Shipley and Mapperley, Derbyshire.

Steam Yacht NARCISSUS

In 1915 the yacht was requisitioned by the British Admiralty for use as an Auxiliary Patrol Vessel, and refitted as an armed yacht, Pendant No 050. She was fitted with two 12 pdr guns. In 1919 the Greek shipping family of Embiricos Brothers acquired the vessel, and on November 18th 1920 she was used to allow former Greek Premier Venizelos to escape from Athens escorted by a Royal Navy cruiser and two destroyers.

During 1925 the steam turbines were removed and replaced by two Sulzer diesel engines at Camper & Nicholson's yard. In 1927 Captain Charles Oswald Liddell of Shirenewton Hall, Monmouth-shire acquired the vessel, and that year she underwent a major refit at Camper & Nicholson.

At the outbreak of World War Two, the *Narcissus* was once again requisitioned by the Royal Navy. She was renamed *HMS Grive* in 1940, equipped with two 12 pounder guns, and carried depth charges. She was commanded by a 67-year-old Captain Lambert, who came out of retirement to perform this duty.

HMS Grive took part in the Dunkirk evacuation of late May 1940 and during three days and nights rescued more than 1,000 men of the British Expeditionary Force. In the early morning of 1st June, while leaving the harbour after an air attack, she struck a mine and sank with the loss of the entire crew of more than 40 apart from one officer, Sub-Lieutenant JK Miles, who was later awarded the DSC. One of the casualties was from Port Henderson, Gairloch.

Owner 1927 to 1939 – Charles Liddell

Charles Oswald Liddell (c. 1854 - 1941) was the head of a trading house which operated in the Far East. He lived and traded in China from 1877 until the early 20th century, and some of his descendants continued in business there until the Communist revolution in the late 1940s made operations difficult.

Charles Liddell was born in Edinburgh. He went out to China in 1877, probably as a soldier. In 1880 he married Elizabeth Kate Birt at the Anglican Cathedral in Shanghai. By this means he inherited Birt's Wharf in Shanghai, where there were go-downs (warehouses), and an active trade in wool, feathers, leather and carpets among other things. He was joined by his brother John and they formed Liddell Bros. The firm thrived in the "wild east" of these days, expanding to Hong Kong, Hankow, Tientsin and Harbin, and making its principals very wealthy.

Loch Broom Men William (surname unconfirmed) on NARCISUSS
(Ullapool Museum)

Having made his fortune, Liddell returned to Britain and bought Shirenewton Hall and estate in Monmouth-shire in about 1901. He established a Japanese garden in the grounds and developed fine collections of Oriental art. Two of his grandsons were decorated in World War Two; the heir to Shirenewton, David Liddell (1917 - 2008), won the Military Cross in Italy in 1943 and his younger brother Ian Oswald Liddell (b. 1920, Shanghai) won a posthumous Victoria Cross in Germany in April 1945.

Norseman

Three Yachts Named Norseman

Loch Broom men serving onboard a yacht named *Norseman* most likely did so in the years from 1877 to 1914. In that period, a Manchester businessman named Samuel Radcliff Platt (1845 - 1902) owned three yachts of that name.

Platt was a Director of the family firm Platt Brothers, which had large engineering works in Lancashire serving the textile industry, and also owned ironworks and collieries. At his death, the company facilities covered over 60 acres and employed nearly 20,000 people. He was Chairman of the Works Committee for the construction of the Manchester Ship Canal.

The naval architect for all three *Norsemen* was St Clare John Byrne (1831-1915), who specialised in designing luxury steam yachts during the late Victorian and early Edwardian period, including the famous *Sunbeam* of 1874 for Thomas Brassey.

The first and second *Norseman* were built by Laird Brothers at Birkenhead in 1877 and 1890, respectively. In 1898, D & W Henderson & Co. of Glasgow built the third *Norseman* (yard number 401). This *Norseman* was a substantial vessel constructed of steel and sported an impressive three-masted barquentine rig. She had a gross tonnage of more than 400 tons and measured about 180 feet in length with a 27ft beam.

The second *Norseman* led the procession to mark the opening of the Manchester Ship Canal in 1894. The image below is from a work by James Mudd, titled *"Opening of the Manchester Ship Canal by the yacht Norseman, 1894 - Owner Mr Platt with the Directors of the Ship Canal on board"*.

Owners after Platt

The second *Norseman* (1890) was sold to an American buyer and passed through a number of US owners before becoming the patrol boat *USS Mohican* in 1917.

When Platt died on board the third *Norseman* in the Menai Strait in 1902, the yacht was sold to Baron Krupp of Kiel, Germany. He also died shortly thereafter, and Mr Laycock of the Royal

Engraving of second NORSEMAN at opening of Manchester Ship Canal
(Wikimedia commons, https://www.flickr.com/photos/manchesterarchiveplus/5209008482/)

Yacht Squadron bought the yacht from Krupp's estate in 1903. After a brief ownership, Laycock sold the yacht to the Earl of Lonsdale in 1904 or 1906.

After Lord Lonsdale sold *Norseman* in 1909, she underwent a brief change of name to *Yreryr* under Welsh ownership, before being bought by William Birtwistle of Preston in 1910 who restored her original name of *Norseman*.

Service after Yachting

During World War One, the third *Norseman* was requisitioned for naval duty and was based at Cherbourg in France for at least part of the conflict. It seems she may have been transferred for further service in Syria in 1920, and then in the Red Sea in 1923.

The vessel seems to have made her way to Italy, where a D. Zolezzi of Savona is noted as owner between 1923 and 1927, and later registered in Genoa in 1932. She seems have been converted for commercial service before 1930 and is recorded as converted to an auxiliary motor schooner in 1939 (i.e. steam engines removed). In 1941, she was reported to have exploded and sunk at Piraeus after catching fire from an adjacent vessel while carrying benzene and explosives from Patras for Rhodes.

Oceana

The Yacht – Early History

Lloyds Register of Yachts lists an *Oceana* as a large wooden schooner of 106 feet length and 21.4 feet beam, built as *Thais* by C Hansen at Cowes in 1880.

Perhaps because she was expensive to run, *Oceana* changed hands regularly. One of her many owners was Sir Percy Florence Shelley, the son of the poet Percy Bysshe Shelley. This Shelley happened to be a friend and neighbour of Robert Louis Stevenson in Bournemouth, and it was he who changed the vessel's name to *Oceana* in tribute to Stevenson as the Scottish author set off to travel the Pacific in 1887.

OCEANA
(GL WATSON)

Oceana was upgraded in 1923 and fitted with two not very powerful engines, although she retained her topsail schooner rig. Even in the early 20th century, she looked somewhat old fashioned with her topsail yards and clipper bow sporting a female figurehead.

At the time of the photograph with the Loch Broom men (1925) the crew jerseys bore the logo RNYC (Royal Northern Yacht Club), as this would have been the club of the then owner Captain Sillars. In the 1930s she was chartered several times by Clinton George Vaughan (1877-1961) of Kent.

Owners

Oceana passed through many hands in her long life, including Gilbert Tonge in 1895 and 1913, James Radley in 1920, Captain Ronald Gordon Sillars from 1923 to 1928, Sir Charles Allom from 1929 to 1933 and Lt Col Benett-Stanford in 1937.

The owner at the time of the 1925 crew photograph was Captain Sillars (1889 - 1969). He owned many different yachts during his life and was based at Shandon, Dumbarton-shire, on the north side of the Clyde. His daughter Fiona (b. 1931) married Adam Kennedy Bergius (1925 - 2017) whose family had married into the Teacher whisky distilling family (described in the *Mariella* section of this book).

Loss of the Oceana

In 1949, the *Oceana* ran aground and broke up on the Baugh end of Crossapol Beach on Tiree under strange circumstances. She had been attempting to reach Sweden from Liverpool to get re-engined in order to be capable of making a journey across the Atlantic with a crew of Latvian asylum seekers.

Onboard were the owner Major John Campbell (1921 - 2015), grandson of the 14th Baron Louth in Ireland, and the group of six Latvians who had chartered the yacht from him. Campbell was a decorated veteran of the British special forces in World War II, and had brought the elderly vessel to Howth near Dublin in 1948. He had met the Latvians in Dublin after they had escaped the Russian occupation of their country by boat and were intent on continuing their journey by sea to the USA.

They ran aground on Tiree during a stormy night in early March due to a navigational error, after they had earlier been forced to call at Liverpool to repair storm damage. They were fortunate not to strike nearby rocks, and although the beach was shallow, the height of the waves made it impossible for them to save themselves. All persons on board were rescued by the Coastguard using breeches buoy.

With daylight it became apparent that the seventy-year-old vessel was damaged beyond repair. A sale of her parts was held on the beach. By the following day, the wreck had almost disappeared under the sand, although some of the frame heads are still visible on the beach at low tide. Some of her fine teak timbers were made into slightly curved fence posts.

Loch Broom Men

Various Loch Broom men were employed on the *Oceana* at one time or another, including Danie "Buie" MacKenzie, John Munro, John MacLeay, and others.

Group of Thirteen on RNYC yacht OCEANA, 1925
(Ullapool Museum)

The photograph shows crew from Gairloch, Letters, Loggie, and Ardindrean. The Lochbroom men include Danie "Buie" MacKenzie (left hand seated), John Munro (second from left standing), J. MacKenzie, Ken MacKay, J. MacPherson, S. MacNab, Duncan Munro, and John MacLeay.

Oriana

The Yacht

Oriana was a 100ft steam yacht, built by the prominent shipbuilding firm of Charles Connell in Glasgow in 1896. She had a Thames measurement of 172 tons and a 31hp engine.

In her early years *Oriana* was listed as owned by a John Gubbins, with Glasgow as her home port. However, a letter to Lochsider Kenneth MacRae in February 1899 mentions that Connell had sold the *Oriana* and would not be able to provide employment for that season, implying that Charles Connell had built the yacht for his own use. Lloyds Register of Yachts for 1899 does show a new owner as Edward Hargreaves.

During World War One this vessel was hired to the Admiralty and served from September 1914 to November 1917. She was equipped with two 3 pdr guns and may have served as a wireless-equipped Auxiliary Patrol Group Leader, at home or in the Mediterranean.

During the 1920s and 1930s, the *Oriana* was owned by Glasgow shipowner Claud Allan.

Steam Yacht
ORIANA
(Alamy)

The Owner – Claud Allan

Claud Allan (1871 - 1945) was a member of the Allan family of Scotland and Canada, owners of the Allan Steamship Line founded by Claud's grandfather in 1819. He was born at 2 Park Gardens, Glasgow, son of Alexander Allan junior. His mother was from the Smith shipping family which controlled the City Line. When Claud's parents died, they left estates of over £500,000 each, enormous sums for the late 1800s.

Claud was a younger brother of Robert S Allan (owner of the steam yacht *Sheila*), and in 1892-3 they formed their own branch of the firm as R & C Allan, based at 121 St Vincent Street, Glasgow. However, by 1917 the Allan Line had lost its independence due to transactions made in Canada. More information on the Allan Line is given in the section on the *Sheila*.

Claud Allan served as a private soldier during the Boer War and was at the siege of Mafeking in 1899-1900. He was later captured and became a prisoner of war. During the First World War he was a initially a member of the Royal Navy Volunteer Reserve, but in 1915 he transferred to the 9th (Glasgow Highland) Battalion of the Highland Light Infantry with the rank of Second Lieutenant, later Captain.

After the First World War, Allan served as a member of Dunbartonshire County Council, and was Deputy Lieutenant of the County, becoming Vice-Lieutenant in 1939.

In addition to his shipping business activities with his brother, Claud Allan became a director of the British Crown Assurance Corporation. In 1932 he was appointed convener of the Finance and Property committee of the Royal Technical College in Glasgow (now Strathclyde University), a post he held until his death.

In his charitable work, he sat on the committee of the Glasgow Mission to the Outdoor Blind and served as its president from 1936 until his death. He was also a trustee of the James Allan Almshouses and the Orphanage at Whiteinch, Glasgow.

Claud Allan was prominent in Clyde yachting circles and became Commodore of the Royal Northern Yacht Club when it was based at Rothesay, and was still at the helm when the club moved to *Ardenvohr* at Rhu in 1937. He was also on the committee of the small and select Mudhook Yacht Club and represented it at the Clyde Yacht Clubs Conference.

From 1908 Claud Allan lived at *Kilmahew*, an impressive 21-bedroom Victorian mansion at Cardross, near Helensburgh on the north side of the Clyde. After his death in 1945, the family sold *Kilmahew* to pay death duties. The house had been damaged during the war when a German land mine aimed for the Clydebank shipyards landed and exploded nearby. In 1948, the property was taken over by the Roman Catholic Church and turned into a seminary. It fell into disuse and was vandalised, eventually being demolished in 1995.

Kilmahew House,
Cardross, home of
Claud Allan owner of
steam yacht ORIANA
- about 1932
(Helensburgh Heritage
Trust)

Ottawa

The Yacht

Ottawa was an early motor cutter fitted with twin screw propulsion, built by McGruer at Clynder in 1912 to a design by GL Watson. She was modestly sized at 54ft long with 12.3ft beam and 34 tons Thames measurement. Her engines were Gardner paraffin type.

The Owner – John Angus

A Mr John Angus of Skelmorlie, Ayrshire owned the *Ottawa* from 1920 until about 1926, covering the period captured in the Loch Broom photograph on page 98.

He had previously owned other yachts, including the 60ft steel steam yacht *Ruby* in 1906 and 1907 (built Denny, Dumbarton in 1888), and the larger steel steam yacht *Volga* in 1908 to 1914. The latter vessel was 95ft long and built by J Reid of Whiteinch, Glasgow in 1896. *Volga* was owned by fishing industry figure George Craig of Aberdeen in 1919.

The Angus family lived in a large house named *Mir-a-Mar* at Skelmorlie, which was used as a hotel in the 1930s and is now converted into separate apartments.

Loch Broom People

The following photograph was taken at the Ardindrean School sports day on 2nd August 1924. All prizes and a picnic were provided by William John Angus whose yachts anchored in Loch Broom for a short time each year.

Picnic at Lochside, 1924
(Ullapool Museum)

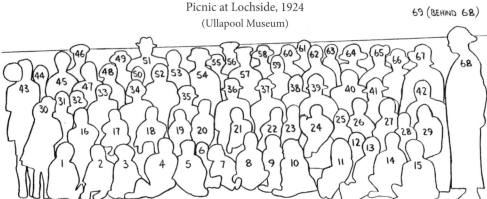

69 (BEHIND 68)

Key Diagram for People in Photograph of Picnic, 1924
(courtesy Finlay "Buie" MacKenzie)

1 Donald MacLeod (James)
2 Reffie MacKenzie (Buie)
3 Sandra MacLennan (daughter of #34 and sister of #18)
4 Kenny MacKenzie (brother of #5 & #6)
5 Evie MacKenzie (brother of #4 & #6)
6 Willie MacKenzie (brother of #4 & #5)
7 Iain MacKenzie (son of #62)
8 Jackie "Buie" MacKenzie (son of #56, brother of #15)
9 John MacKenzie, Southend
10 Peggy MacIntyre (MacLean)
11 Betty MacKenzie
12 Katie Ann Rose
13 Christopher Munro
14 John MacKay Rose
15 Roddy "Buie" MacKenzie (son of #56, brother of #8)
18 Murdo MacLennan (son of #34 and brother of #3)
21 Joey MacKenzie (daughter of #36)
22 Roddy (or Finlay) MacKenzie (Tor twin, son of #37)
23 Iain MacKenzie (Tor – son of #37)
24 Murdo Simon MacKenzie (son of #39)
25 Meg MacKenzie, Loggie (twin)
26 Norman MacLean (son of #41)
27 John Alec Maclean (son of #41)
28 Iain MacKenzie, Loggie (twin)
29 Donald Rose (son of #42)
34 Mrs Annie MacLennan, Letters
36 Mrs Bella MacKenzie, Rhiroy
37 Mrs Robina MacKenzie, Tor (wife of John "Onorach")
38 Mary MacKenzie (Braes)
39 Mrs Chrissie MacKenzie (Allan)

40 Jessie MacKenzie, Loggie
41 Mrs Jessack MacLean, Loggie
42 Maggie Rose, Letters
43 Alick "Lally" MacKenzie, Rhiroy
44 Johnnie MacLean, Ardindrean (Clane)
45 Flora MacKenzie (MacNab)
46 Possibly engineer of the yacht
47 Nana Munro, Ardcharnich
48 Joan MacRae, Loggie
49 Mrs Mary MacNab
50 Annabella Skinner (MacNab)
51 Major Fraser, Leckmelm
52 Peggy MacLeod, Rhiroy
53 Mrs Annie MacKenzie, Letters (Aunta, wife of old Finlay "Buie")
56 Captain John "Buie" MacKenzie, Letters (husband of #66, father of #8 & #15)
57 Mr Angus (yacht owner)
58 Meg MacKenzie, Letters (Buie)
59 Annie MacKenzie (James)
60 Isa Munro, Ardcharnich
61 Mrs Johan MacLean
62 Mrs Maggie MacKenzie (teacher)
63 Roddy MacKenzie
64 Katie MacKenzie
65 Rae MacKenzie, Loggie (Buie)
66 Mrs Isabella MacKenzie, Letters (Buie, wife of #56)
67 Mrs Jessie MacKenzie, Letters (wife of Dan Buie)
68 Mrs Bella MacNab
69 Annie MacNab (daughter of #68, hiding behind #68)

The yacht was skippered by John Mackenzie (Buie) of Letters, an uncle of Duncan MacKenzie (Tor). John "Buie" can be seen in the centre of the group behind William Angus, both men in yachting uniform. Major Fraser of Leckmelm (killed in France, 1940) is the gentleman wearing a hat. Mr Angus also made provision for Christmas parties for the school-children each year. This continued for at least 30 years. Afterwards, the practice was continued by Sir Michael Peto of Dundonnell Estate until the school closed.

Panope

The Yacht & Owners

Panope was a successful racing and cruising yacht built in 1928 by Camper & Nicholson in Gosport to a design by Alfred Mylne (design no. 314).

She was a large two-masted gaff schooner, 97ft long on deck with a beam of 19ft and a draft of 12ft. Originally, *Panope* had a sail area of 4,500 ft^2, and was fitted with a small 17hp Bergius paraffin engine.

This yacht was originally built for Captain John Duckworth Hodgson DFC, a decorated aviator with the Royal Flying Corps in World War One. He owned her until about 1938, when he moved on to the slightly larger steel schooner *Panda* (Mylne design no. 387).

PANOPE
under sail

Panope's new owner was Brigadier George Clark, who kept her until after World War Two. Thereafter she went through several owners and name changes (*Candide, Velella II, Doudouna, Lily III*) and moved overseas. She is believed to have been lost in a hurricane in the 1970s.

Loch Broom Men

Although not strictly from Lochbroom, Roddy MacLean from Inverasdale worked on the *Panope* and later lived in Ullapool. His details are given in the following chapter.

Pelagia

The Yacht

Lloyds Register of Yachts for 1906-07 lists a *Pelagia* as owned by Mr CJ Morgan and based at Southampton. This *Pelagia* was a wooden yawl with 3,088 ft^2 sail area, built by Whites of Southampton in 1903 to the order of Mr Morgan and designed by the famous Fred Shepherd. She had a length on deck of 72ft (length over spars 92ft), a beam of 13'2" and a draft of 8'9".

In the early 21st century she was reported to have been discovered abandoned in Guadeloupe, by an Italian art historian and collector. As far as is known, the old *Pelagia* still awaits a new owner willing and able to undertake a huge and expensive restoration.

Owners

Some owners listed by Lloyds include T G Wotherspoon (1913 to 1922), Major Alan Swinton (1933) and Archibald Watson (1927 to 1931).

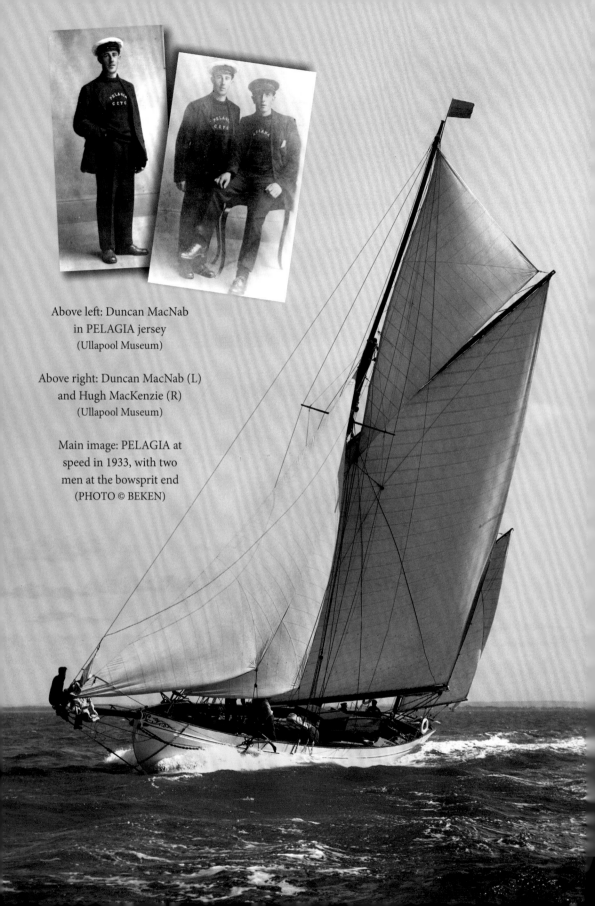

Above left: Duncan MacNab
in PELAGIA jersey
(Ullapool Museum)

Above right: Duncan MacNab (L)
and Hugh MacKenzie (R)
(Ullapool Museum)

Main image: PELAGIA at
speed in 1933, with two
men at the bowsprit end
(PHOTO © BEKEN)

TG Wotherspoon was a member of the family which controlled the Glenfield Starch Works at Paisley. He employed West Highland men in his yacht crews, including Skipper Angus MacPherson of Skye (b. Ullapool, 1859).

Archibald Watson could also have been the owner at the time of the Loch Broom men's involvement. He was a member of the Clyde Corinthian Yacht Club, and lived at the fine Glasgow address of 9 Montgomerie Drive, Kelvinside (now renamed as Cleveden Drive).

World War Two appears to have brought major ownership changes. The yacht was still named *Pelagia* and owned in the UK in 1939 but reappears in Lloyds Register in 1947 renamed as *L'Inconnue* and owned by Prince Ismail Hassan. In 1952 *Pelagia* belonged to a Mr E Maza Y Garay at Alexandria, Egypt, who then appears with the boat based at Villefranche on the Cote d'Azur in 1960. After that, the trail gets colder. There are reports that she was at one stage renamed *Diogene* and owned by high profile individuals including members of the Bugatti and Farouk families.

Loch Broom Men

One of the photographs opposite shows Duncan MacNab of Letters in a *Pelagia* jersey together with Hugh MacKenzie of Ardindrean from the steam yacht *Ariana*. Hugh (Huisdean) was the father of Kate Rettie and her brothers Andrew, Jock "the Hod" and Tommy MacKenzie.

This is a studio photograph and would most probably have been taken in the late 1920s, when both *Pelagia* and the *Ariana* (owned by Thomas Dunlop) were based in the Clyde area.

Rionnag na Mara

The Yacht

Rionnag na Mara (Star of the Sea) was a large steam yacht of 310 tons Thames measurement, built in 1886 by John Reid at Port Glasgow.

She was constructed of steel with a length of 153ft. The steam engine was of an unusual six cylinder quadruple expansion type. Her owner Pirie was an industrialist, interested in steam technology because of the power demands of his paper manufacturing business. The plant installed on the *Rionnag na Mara* was one of the first high-pressure steam installations for marine work, operating at the then high pressure of 180 pounds per square inch. This engine was featured in several British and foreign mechanical engineering periodicals of the time.

The yacht was used for several long voyages, including to the coasts of Norway and to Russia. It was said that one of her crew encountered another Loch Broom man on the streets of Vladivostok. This seems rather far-fetched, but could have been possible if the vessel completed

RIONNAG NA MARA as Poupee under French ownership

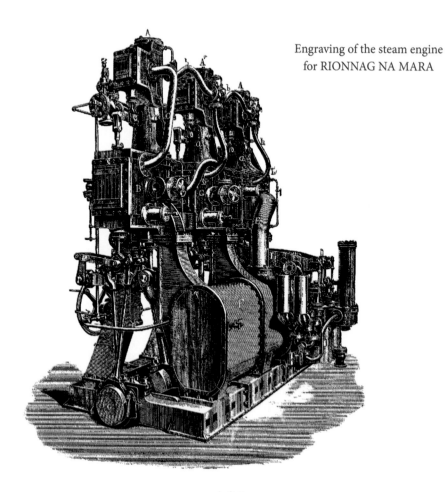

Engraving of the steam engine
for RIONNAG NA MARA

Towing the Reid built Iron Church into Loch Sunart, 1846

a round-the-world voyage. More likely is that St Petersburg or Archangelsk was the location of this meeting of Gaels.

Pirie sold *Rionnag na Mara* in the 1890s, and by 1899 she was in France. Her owner Prince de Nissole was one of the early aviation pioneers. During World War One the vessel served in the French Navy and was present at the Dardanelles in 1915. Her names in France were *L'Aigle*, *Poupette*, and *Poupée*. She is believed to have been scrapped in 1929.

The Builder (John Reid)

John Reid & Company was a shipbuilding firm, originally based at Port Glasgow on the lower Clyde, but latterly at Whiteinch in Glasgow.

The Port Glasgow business operated from 1847 to 1891, and one of its first contracts was the "crowd-funded" Floating Church built in 1846 for the Loch Sunart congregation of the newly formed Free Church. William Lithgow (later to run his own shipyard) trained as an apprentice ship draughtsman at this yard.

Later (from 1891 to 1909) the business operated from Whiteinch in Glasgow, under the control of James Reid. It was during this period that they built the *Carraig* (later the steam yacht of Sir James Lithgow) and the four-masted barque *Mneme* of 1903, now preserved as the *Pommern* museum ship at Mariehamn in the Aland Islands.

In 1909 the yard was taken over and absorbed by Barclay, Curle and Co Ltd.

The Owner – Alexander Pirie

During the late 19th century *Rionnag na Mara* was commissioned and owned by a man well known to the Loch Broom men as a local landlord. This was Alexander George Pirie (1836 – 1904), notorious for carrying out some of the last land clearances on the Scottish mainland. These took place at Leckmelm, across the loch from Letters and Ardindrean, in 1880.

Pirie purchased the property in 1879 and soon set about transforming Leckmelm into a model estate. Unhappily, his plans for improving the estate involved depriving the tenants of the use of the land, and later removing them from their cottages.

His factor Gauld was instructed to give the tenants the option to give up their livestock and crops and stay and work for Pirie - or leave. As a result, some families moved to the other side of the loch, where the land was steep and difficult to cultivate, while others chose to emigrate.

The famous notice, dated 2nd November 1879, reads as follows;

> *I am instructed by Mr Pirie, proprietor of Leckmelm, to give you notice that the present arrangements by which you hold the cottage, byre, and other buildings, together with lands on that estate, will cease from and after the term of Martinmas, 1880; and further, I am instructed to intimate to you that at the said term of Martinmas, 1880, Mr Pirie purposes taking the whole arable and pasture lands, but that he is desirous of making arrangements whereby you may continue tenant of the cottage upon terms and conditions yet to be settled upon.*
>
> *I have further to inform you that unless you and the other tenants at once prevent your sheep and other stock from grazing or trespassing upon the enclosures and hill, and other lands now in the occupation or possession of the said Mr Pirie, he will not, upon any conditions, permit you to remain in the cottage you now occupy, after the said term of Martinmas, 1880, but will clear all off the estate, and take down the cottages.*

Pirie's actions caused dissent locally which became part of a national debate. John MacMillan, the local Free Church minister, publicised the events and John Murdoch's *Highlander* newspaper supported the crofters' case. The Leckmelm dispute helped fuel the Highland Land War or Crofters' War which led in March 1883 to the establishment of the Royal Commission of Inquiry into the Condition of the Crofters and Cottars in the Highlands & Islands of Scotland (the Napier Commission). In summer 1883 the Commission took evidence from Pirie and his tenants, amongst others, and published its findings in 1884. This led to the Crofting Act of 1886 which finally gave crofters security of tenure. However, the Leckmelm crofters never got their holdings back. Pirie's legacy means that Leckmelm is one of the few estates in the area which has no crofted land. The remains of some of the former houses can still be seen above the main A835 road.

Despite the negative publicity, Pirie proceeded with his plans. He created a large home farm complex with estate cottages and gardens and did provide employment for local people on the farm, in the gardens and on his yachts. One of his first actions was to take down most of the dykes and convert the long, narrow strips of land into fields which could be more easily worked. In Pirie's opinion, without these changes the land could not have been ploughed or farmed properly.

In 1884, he took an apparently vindictive case to the Court of Session against Hugh Rose from Letters across the loch, seeking an interdict against the crofter cutting or removing seaweed from between the high and low water marks on the shore at Leckmelm. In his evidence to the Napier Commission in 1883, Pirie had gone to great pains to explain how poor (in his opinion) seaweed was as a fertiliser.

Pirie inherited his wealth from the family paper manufacturing business, operating at Stoneywood, Aberdeen from 1770, and under the control of the Pirie's since 1800. With an abundant supply of running fresh water in the Dee and Don rivers, Aberdeen was a major centre for paper making well into the 20th century. Water is fundamental to paper-making, as an integral part of the process, and previously as the motive power for driving the machines. The lower reaches of the River Don were once lined with 17 mills.

Pirie's grandfather Alexander (1778 - 1860) had been responsible for much of the growth of the company in the early 19th century. The young Alexander joined the firm in 1856, but when his father Francis (1809 – 1870) died he withdrew to pursue other interests, including country estates and yachting. Francis had owned a Fife built 45 ton yawl (*Lena*, 1867) and this vessel was still owned by the family in 1880. Prior to the *Rionnag na Mara*, Alexander Pirie had the small steam yacht *Whaup* (95ft, 76 tons Thames measurement), built by Dobson & Charles at Grangemouth in 1882. In 1900 and 1902 he had a small (27 feet long) cutter named *Floating Feather*.

A business crisis in 1891 (the year *Rionnag na Mara* was sold) brought Pirie back to lead the family firm. Following his death in 1904, Leckmelm passed to Frank Calvert (owner of *The Ketch*). In 1922 the Pirie firm was merged with Wiggins Teape, which continues today in the paper business.

Loch Broom Men

Kenneth MacKenzie (Coinneach an Onorach) grandfather of Duncan "Tor" MacKenzie and great-grandfather of Sandy Mackenzie worked on this yacht. Other Loch Broom seamen were also employed by Pirie, including Angus MacIntyre, Rhue, and John MacKenzie, grandfather of MacNab MacKenzie (b. 1931).

Upper: Two sons of Alexander Pirie with brother in law Viscount Selby
(Ullapool Museum)

Above: Estate workers and residents at launching of small Pirie yacht at Leckmelm
(Ullapool Museum)

Right: Small Pirie yacht at Leckmelm
(Ullapool Museum)

Painting of small and large yacht (believed to depict RIONNAG NA MARA) at Leckmelm
(Mortimer Gibbs, 1887, Ullapool Museum)

Roska

The Yacht

Roska was a large auxiliary gaff ketch built on the Clyde in 1930 by Bute Slip Dock Co. to a design by yard owner Alfred Mylne. She was Mylne design No 328, and was 75ft deck length, 51ft on the waterline, 15.75ft beam, with a draught of 9.75ft. Originally, *Roska* had a four cylinder 28-30 Gleniffer paraffin engine.

She was constructed of 1.75" teak planking on timber frames of 3.87" siding and 5.25 to 3.87" moulded depth, spaced every 17.25". The beam stringer was 5" x 6" pitch pine, and the normal deck beams were oak of 3" x 3" to 4.5" x 3" (heavier in way of the masts).

First Owner – MacGeorge

The first owner of *Roska* was Mr AM MacGeorge (1887 - 1959), a Glasgow stockbroker. Andrew Morrison MacGeorge had previously owned the yacht *Valentine*, which was still present on the Clyde in 1937 and is mentioned elsewhere in this book.

Left: ROSKA under sail
(Kate Rettie photo)

Right: ROSKA at anchor
(MacGregor photo)

Opposite: General
Arrangement of ROSKA
(courtesy of Mylne Yacht Design)

The MacGeorges were a long established family connected with land ownership in the south of Scotland. Glasgow Cathedral has a stained glass window in their memory, erected by Andrew MacGeorge in 1951. Andrew's grandfather was one of the founders of the Institute of Accountants & Actuaries of Glasgow in 1854, which became part of the Institute of Chartered Accountants of Scotland (ICAS) in 1951. Andrew MacGeorge's uncle Bernard Buchanan MacGeorge was a serious art collector whose collection included works by James Whistler and William Blake. In 1905 he sold a set of four Shakespeare Folios for the sum of £10,000 (today worth about £1 million).

In 1930, Lloyds Register of Yachts listed Andrew MacGeorge's address as 24 George Square, Glasgow probably the address of his firm Penney & MacGeorge. His home address was 20 Woodside Terrace, Glasgow, near his uncle Bernard MacGeorge at No. 19 and William Wylie (owner of *Vida VI*) at No. 13. The yacht was recorded as attached to the port of Greenock.

As well as owning *Roska* in the 1930s, he was also the first owner of a Rolls Royce Barker saloon, first shown at the Barcelona Motor Show of 1935, and still in existence today.

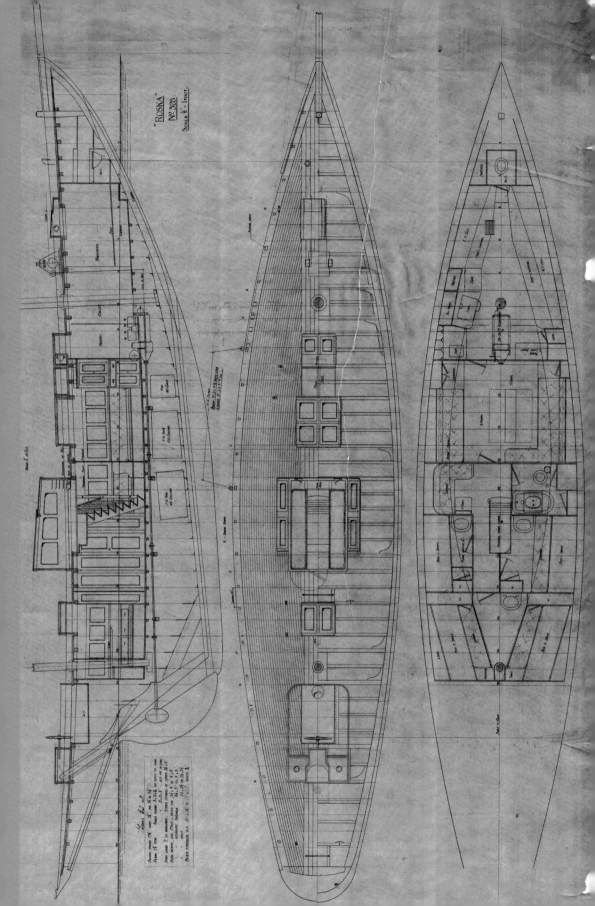

"ROSKA"
Nº 328
SCALE ⅜" = 1 FOOT.

ROSKA as AROSA under Spanish flag with Bermudan rig
(photo reproduced courtesy of Spanish Navy)

Left: Andrew MacGeorge's home at 20 Woodside Terrace, Glasgow – pictured in 21st Century

Right: Andrew MacGeorge's 1935 Rolls-Royce 20/25 Barker Saloon

Subsequent Owners

After MacGeorge's death in 1959, *Roska* was owned for most of the 1960s by a Hamilton Marr of Greenock, and in 1961 she was converted from gaff to Bermudan rig, at a reported cost of £10,000. In the late 1960s *Roska* was sold to William Lawrence of Helensburgh, a friend of Ullapool's Angie "Allan" MacKenzie.

The Lawrences renamed her *Charm of Rhu II* and modified the propeller and gearbox. Together with a service of the old engine this finally allowed the vessel to motor into wind and sea. With the original installation, the boat would stop dead even at full throttle when heading into anything approaching a gale. Under sail, *Roska* is reported to have been fast enough to overtake a Clyde steamer.

The Lawrences sold her in the late 1970s. Since 1981 the yacht has worked as a Spanish Navy school ship, based in North West Spain. She is named *Arosa* and normally sails with two officers and 12 seamen. Before working as a Navy school ship, the yacht had the name *Algoma* and is believed to have been seized following operations against drug trafficking in the Canary Islands.

The Designer - Alfred Mylne

Alfred Mylne (1872-1951) was a prominent Scottish yacht designer. He was born in Glasgow and initially apprenticed to the Scottish shipbuilders Napier, Shanks and Bell, and then worked as a draftsman and apprentice to GL Watson. Watson was famous as the designer of *Britannia*, the racing cutter first owned by Edward, Prince of Wales.

Mylne set up his own office in 1896 at the age of 24. In 1906, he was involved in establishing the International Metre Rule, a yacht-racing handicap rule. Mylne designed a number of race-winning yachts, including the 19-Metre class cutter *Octavia* in 1911. His firm [1,2] was also responsible for the design of other classic yachts featured in this book, such as *Thendara* (1937) and *Vadura* (1926).

The Stephens of Linthouse history states that the four ketches built at Stephen's yard in the 1930s (*Golden Hind, Fiumara, Albyn, Thendara*) were designed by JM James of the Alfred Mylne firm [7].

Together with his brother Charles, Alfred took over the Bute Slip Dock yard at Port Bannatyne in 1911, which then built boats to his designs and the designs of others. This yard is still in operation today as the Ardmaleish Boatyard.

He retired in 1945 and handed the Glasgow design office and the Bute yard over to his nephew Alfred Mylne the Second. The Bute yard passed out of Mylne ownership in 1975. The design firm continues today under new ownership and markets material from the old archives.

Loch Broom Men

Roska was active for nearly ten years before World War Two, in a period when photography was becoming more available to ordinary people. Her crew changed over that period, and as a result of these factors *Roska* and a variety of crew members are among the best represented in this book.

Crew of ROSKA – late 1930s
Left to Right; John "Onorach" MacKenzie, William MacGregor (Scoraig), John MacLean (Ardindrean), Kenny "Skene" MacKenzie, skipper William MacKenzie (Rhiroy)
(Ullapool Museum)

Crewman at bowsprit end on
ROSKA – Hugh "Huisdean"
MacKenzie, Ardindrean
(Christine Harvey photo)

Above left: Relaxing beside cockpit on ROSKA - John MacLean & John "Onorach" MacKenzie
(Christine Harvey photo)

Below left: ROSKA crew – including Duncan MacNab & John MacLean
(back centre), skipper W. MacKenzie (back right)
(Ullapool Museum)

Below right: (L) Duncan MacNab, (R) Donald "James" Macleod, both Ardindrean
(Ullapool Museum)

Above left: ROSKA crew – Kenny "Skene", skipper W. MacKenzie, Duncan MacNab, "Polson" from Gairloch
(Ullapool Museum)

Above right: ROSKA crew – (L) John MacLean, (R) I. MacKenzie (Rhiroy)
(Ullapool Museum)

Below left: (L) Kenny "Sgean" MacKenzie, (R) William MacGregor on ROSKA – late 1930s
(MacGregor photo)

Below right: Crew on ROSKA – L to R; John "Clane" MacLean, Unknown, Roddy "Buie" MacKenzie
(MacGregor photo)

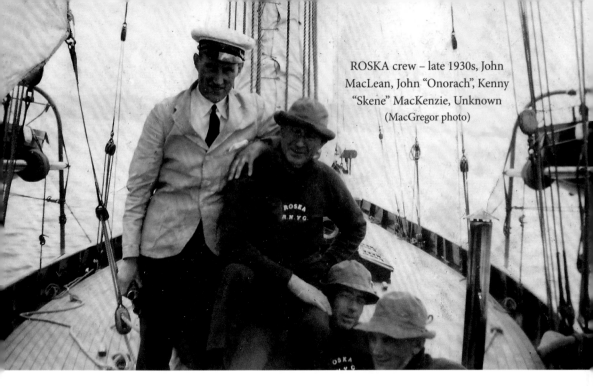

ROSKA crew – late 1930s, John MacLean, John "Onorach", Kenny "Skene" MacKenzie, Unknown (MacGregor photo)

Left: Crew and Guests onboard ROSKA – probably early 1930s (Kate Rettie photo)

Right: Crew on ROSKA enjoying strong refreshment – late 1930s – Roddie "Buie" MacKenzie on left (MacGregor photo)

Satellite

The Yacht

In Lloyds Register of Yachts for 1895 three *Satellites* are listed, but only one is based on the Clyde. The RCYC on the jerseys makes it virtually certain that the Loch Broom men served onboard the William Fife designed yawl *Satellite*, built at Fairlie in 1852. She was originally 68 feet long overall and 15.7 feet beam, but around 1877 she seems to have been lengthened to 77 feet at Dartmouth.

From 1880 to 1900, this yacht was owned in Sligo and County Down in Ireland. In 1895 Lloyds Register of Yachts shows the owner as Mr G Herbert Brown (Helen's Bay, County Down) but the home port is given as Glasgow. By 1905, she made her last appearance in Lloyds, and the executors of a Walter Hatton of Edinburgh are recorded as the owners of this elderly boat.

Loch Broom Men

Group on board RCYC yacht SATELLITE - Front centre Duncan MacNab, Ardindrean
(Ullapool Museum)

116

Sheila

The Yacht

Sheila was a very popular name for yachts, with no fewer than twelve listed in the 1930 Lloyds Register of Yachts, ignoring the *Sheila II's* etc.

The ship's lifebelt which Lally (Alec Mackenzie) is holding in one of the photographs identifies the vessel as a SY, or Steam Yacht. In the 1930 Lloyds Register of Yachts there are two very similar steam yachts listed. They were both small, with particulars as follows;

- *Sheila* – Steel construction, steam yacht with schooner rig, 23hp, 80 feet LOA, built 1904 by Whites at Cowes. Owned in 1930 by Robert S Allan LL.D, a Glasgow based ship owner.
- *Sheila* – Composite construction, steam yacht with schooner rig, 11hp, 79 feet LOA, built 1893 by Whites at Cowes. Owned in 1930 by R O Evans, a Welshman.

The Glasgow ownership, and the fact that Robert Allan was a senior officer of the Clyde Corinthian Yacht Club and the Royal Clyde Yacht Club, make it virtually certain that Lally was employed on the 1904 built steel vessel.

SHEILA
(GL WATSON)

Robert Allan kept this yacht from 1923 until his death in 1932. In 1933 she was owned by an A B MacIntosh and in 1937 by a Mr Glynn Terrell.

The Owner – Robert Allan

Robert Smith Allan (1857–1932) was a well-known Glasgow shipowner and educational administrator, and the older brother of Claud Allan, owner of the steam yacht *Oriana*. The brothers were third-generation members of the family which controlled the famous Allan Line, and in 1892-3 formed their own branch of the firm as R&C Allan (shipowners), based at 121 St Vincent Street, Glasgow. The Allan Line was sold to the Canadian Pacific company in 1909.

Robert's grandfather, Captain Alexander Allan (1780–1854) founded the Allan shipping business in 1819. The firm traded principally between the UK and the Americas, especially Canada. Robert's father, Alexander junior (1825–1892) was senior partner in the J & A Allan branch of the firm. Robert's mother came from the shipping family of George Smith, owners of the large City Line, in which Robert became a partner.

In addition to his shipping business, Robert S Allan was also a director of the African Lakes Corporation, with interests in Nyasaland (Malawi) during and after the First World War.

He was genuinely interested in education, and joined the Glasgow School Board as finance convenor in 1894, becoming Board Chairman in 1903. In addition, he chaired Glasgow's Teacher Training and Secondary Education Committees, worked with mentally-disabled children's charities, and sat on the Glasgow & West of Scotland (later Royal) Technical College Board from 1900 to 1931.

Robert S Allan was a keen campaigner against alcohol abuse and a promoter of total abstinence. It is not recorded how these preferences were regarded by his crews.

The Allan Line

The Allan Shipping Line was founded in 1819 by Captain Alexander Allan of Saltcoats, Ayrshire, trading between Scotland and Montreal. By the 1830s the company had offices in Glasgow, Liverpool and Montreal.

All five of Captain Allan's sons were actively involved with the shipping business. In 1854, Captain Allan's second son Hugh (1810 - 1882) based himself in Canada and created the Montreal Ocean Steamship Company as part of the Allan Line. Two years later he displaced Cunard to take over the Royal Mail contract between Britain and North America.

The Allan Line transported millions of Scottish and other European emigrants to North America, many to Canada. By the 1880s, it was the largest privately owned merchant fleet in the

Allan Line advertising poster
(Alamy)

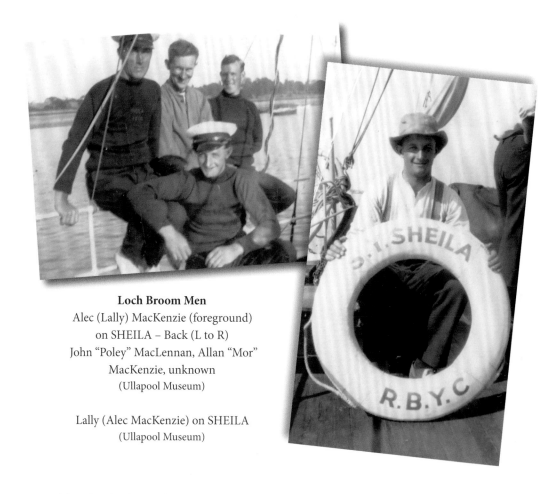

Loch Broom Men
Alec (Lally) MacKenzie (foreground)
on SHEILA – Back (L to R)
John "Poley" MacLennan, Allan "Mor"
MacKenzie, unknown
(Ullapool Museum)

Lally (Alec MacKenzie) on SHEILA
(Ullapool Museum)

world. At his death, Hugh Allan was one of the world's richest men, with a fortune estimated to be in the region of ten million pounds.

The company took over the State Line in 1891 and from then was often referred to as the Allan & State Line. In 1897, Hugh's brother Andrew Allan (1822 - 1901) amalgamated the various branches of the Allan shipping business under one company, Allan Line Steamship Company Ltd., of Glasgow.

Hugh's Canadian son Sir Montagu Allan (1860 – 1951) represented the third and last generation of the Allan family to control this large business. In the period around 1909, the Allan Line was sold to the competing Canadian Pacific Steamships, and Montagu Allan retired from shipping in 1912. For reasons still not understood, the sale was kept secret until announced in parliament in 1915. The merged company became known as Canadian Pacific Ocean Services Limited, and by 1917 the Allan Line flag had disappeared from commercial shipping.

Sonamara

The Yacht

Sonamara was a small wooden twin screw motor yacht, fitted with two masts. She was designed and built in 1936 by Hugh MacLean of Renfrew with two paraffin Thornycroft engines (by 1950 these had been changed to Ailsa Craig diesel engines). Her Thames measurement was 35 tons, and she was 48ft overall length with a beam of 14.5ft.

Although her port was given as Glasgow, she seems to have been owned from the time of her build into the 1950s by an Alexander MacCulloch with an address in Berkshire.

Loch Broom Men

Donald "James" MacLeod from Ardindrean worked on *Sonamara*. He was the father of Isobel MacKenzie (first wife of Duncan "Tor" MacKenzie).

Southern Cross

The Yachts

The famous railway engineer Sir John Fowler had several steam yachts named *Southern Cross*. From 1880 to 1886 he owned a vessel built in 1878 by JS White at Cowes, Isle of Wight. This yacht was 98.5ft long and 16.5ft beam with 119 tons Thames measurement and a 30hp steam engine.

Donald MacLeod, Ardindrean
on SONAMARA
(Ullapool Museum)

In 1888, he had a much larger vessel, built in 1876 by Lobnitz at Renfrew on the Clyde. This vessel was constructed of iron with a Thames measurement of 332 tons and a 60hp steam engine. She was 161ft long with a beam of 21.1ft. With this vessel, Fowler cruised the Mediterranean including the Greek islands. In July 1889 this *Southern Cross* went aground on a rock in Loch Slapin, Skye. A tug was dispatched from the Clyde to assist.

In 1897, shortly before he died, Fowler had another *Southern Cross*, this time smaller and more suitable for the narrow bays and channels of the Scottish west coast. This vessel was 82ft long

Steam yacht SOUTHERN CROSS moored in Loch Broom just south of Ardcharnich in 1886
(photo courtesy Peter Newling)

with a 14ft beam and a Thames measurement of 71 tons. She was built in 1886 by Cochrane at Birkenhead with a 30hp engine.

The Owner – Sir John Fowler

Sir John Fowler (1817 to 1898) was one of the great engineers of the Victorian age. During the 1850s and 1860s, he was engineer for the world's first underground transport system; London's Metropolitan Railway. In the 1880s, in partnership with Benjamin Baker, he was chief engineer for the gigantic Forth Railway Bridge project.

Fowler was born in Wadsley, Sheffield, to land surveyor John Fowler and his wife Elizabeth. The pioneering Stockton and Darlington railway line opened when Fowler was eight years of age, and it was perhaps not surprising that he should gravitate towards railway work. After gaining experience, Fowler initially established a practice as a consulting engineer in the Yorkshire and Lincolnshire area, but moved to London in 1844. In 1850 he married Elizabeth Broadbent. They had four sons.

In 1853, Fowler became chief engineer of the Metropolitan Railway in London. He was also engineer for the District Railway and the Hammersmith & City Railway. Today these works form the majority of London Underground's Circle Line and related routes. For this work, he demanded huge fees of several hundred thousand pounds – worth tens of millions of pounds today. Sir Edward Watkin, chairman of the Metropolitan Railway, complained, *"No engineer in the world was so highly paid"*.

John Fowler and Benjamin Baker designed and engineered the huge Forth Bridge shortly after the Tay Bridge had collapsed in 1879. Fowler focused on the masonry approach viaducts while Baker dealt mainly with the steel structure. Construction of the bridge began in 1882 and when it opened in 1890 it had the longest single cantilever span of any bridge in the world. The bridge was the first major structure in Britain to be constructed of steel. Its French contemporary, the Eiffel Tower (completed 1889), was built with the older wrought iron material.

In 1865 and 1867 Fowler purchased country estates totalling 40,000 acres at Braemore and Inverbroom, near Ullapool. He was a regular visitor to Loch Broom over the following three decades. Using local blue gneiss and Glasgow sandstone, he built the impressive Braemore House (now demolished) on a hillside 700 feet above sea level. During these years, he applied his wealth and engineering skills to develop the estate, planting a huge number of trees and creating a local hydro-electric power scheme.

The Fowler Memorial Clock in Ullapool was erected in 1899 in memory of Sir John Arthur Fowler and his family. The clock was originally located in the middle of the street at the junction of Quay Street and Argyle Street. In the 1960s it was moved from the road to the street corner because of complaints about traffic congestion. Fowler's eldest son John Arthur died shortly after his father in 1899, and his two sons Alan and John Edward (Sir John's grandsons) lost their lives in World War One. Commemorative plaques were added to the clock in their honour.

Fowler Memorial Clock, Ullapool (cc-by-sa/2.0 - © Leslie Barrie - geograph.org. uk/p/3361922)

The Ketch

The Yacht

This unimaginatively named yacht was built in 1906 by William Fife of Fairlie. She was originally a large engineless ketch of 87ft length and 19.3ft beam with a Thames measurement of 111 tons. By 1910 she had two Gardner paraffin engines installed.

The Owners

The Ketch was originally built for Kenneth Mackenzie Clark (1868–1932). He was a member of the extremely wealthy Clark thread-making family of Paisley, which is described more fully in

THE KETCH
(Diyanne Ross photo)

the chapter on *Vadura*. Clark bought and sold many yachts in quick succession over the years (*Kentra* is another example), and he kept *The Ketch* for only a few years before selling her to Frank Calvert of Ashton Park, Preston in about 1909.

Calvert was a Lancashire mill owner born about 1862. He owned many other yachts and several properties, including Leckmelm estate on the north side of Loch Broom, following the notorious Pirie. Calvert was proprietor for only a short time before dying at Leckmelm in 1915 while fishing at one of the freshwater lochs from a collapsible canvas boat. He was believed to have suffered a heart attack and fallen into the water. His gamekeeper or ghillie was present on the bank but unable to help as he could not swim.

As Calvert was unmarried, the Leckmelm estate was bequeathed to his factor Major Fraser, and *The Ketch* was passed to a female relative. Constance Calvert was born in 1880 and married a Hugh Riddell in 1912. She lived in Lancashire and is recorded as the owner of *The Ketch* throughout the 1920s and 1930s.

The history of *The Ketch* during World War One and Two is not known. By 1947 she is listed as belonging to a Charles Alexander. Throughout this period her home port was given as Glasgow, but by 1963 she was registered as owned in Greece.

Loch Broom Men

Murdo MacLean from Ardindrean worked on this vessel in 1930 with Peter Stewart as Skipper. Duncan MacPherson from Gairloch (grandfather of Diyanne Ross from Coigach) sailed on *The Ketch* and also on the *Eileen*.

Murdo MacLean reference from service on THE KETCH, 1930
(courtesy Ian & Murdo MacLean)

Thendara (1937)

The Owner

Arthur Stewart Leslie Young (1899 - 1950) was a Scottish Conservative & Unionist politician and businessman. He sat as the Member of Parliament for Glasgow Partick from 1935 to 1945, and then for Glasgow Scotstoun until his death in 1950. During the Second World War he held junior ministerial posts in the Coalition Government of 1940-1945 and the Caretaker Government of 1945. Perhaps as an acknowledgement of this public service, he was created a baronet in September 1945. One of his homes was Auchentoshan at Dalmuir on the north side of the Clyde.

Young was a keen yachtsman, racing 8-Metres and Dragons, and a member of the Clyde Corinthian Yacht Club, of which he was Commodore in 1949. As well as owning *Thendara* he was responsible for ordering a number of racing boats at Fife of Fairlie, including the 8-Metre class *Saskia* (1930), the 6-Metres *Saga* (1925) and *Saskia II* (1933), and the 18ft *Minette* (1932). He also owned the Dragon *Ta-Yen* (McGruer, 1938).

Arthur Young's financial independence derived from the Templeton carpet manufacturing family, to which his mother belonged. This firm occupied a distinctive factory near Glasgow Green, modelled on the Moorish-Italian style of the Doge's Palace in Venice. The business was established by James Templeton, born in Campbeltown in 1802.

A.S.L. Young was a son of Daniel Henderson Lusk Young, who had started work at the firm in 1884. At the end of 1887 Daniel was promoted to partnership, and within a year of that date, he married a daughter of John S. Templeton. Gradually his control extended over all branches of the business. During the First World War, D.H.L. Young supervised the diversion of the factory into the manufacture of blankets for the army and other war work. In 1921 he died, and his brother F.H. Young (died 1943) became senior partner in the business. A.S.L. Young took over control of the Axminster factory division in 1918, at a young age, later becoming Chairman.

Sir Arthur Young died from a heart attack when onboard *Thendara* in Brittany in 1950. To avoid bureaucratic complications, his widow had the yacht immediately sailed home to Scotland with the body onboard.

Templeton factory in Glasgow – now a business park
(cc-by-sa/2.0 - © Carol Walker - geograph.org.uk/p/1688682)

The Yacht

In 1936 Arthur Young asked Alfred Mylne to design him a large and seaworthy racing cruiser. *Thendara* (design number 379) was completed in April 1937 by the Clydeside shipbuilding yard of Alexander Stephen and Sons and was one of the last cruising yachts to be constructed before World War Two.

Stephen of Linthouse was a shipyard which primarily produced large merchant ships, but also built fine yachts, including several designed by the Alfred Mylne firm. According to Sandy Stephen's memoirs, when *Thendara* was launched she stuck halfway down the launch ways [8]. The Linthouse ways were designed to be suitable for much larger and heavier ships, and this difficulty was not unexpected. A winch pulled *Thendara* part way back up the slip, from where she was again released to finally glide into the water.

The figures recorded in the Stephen's records for *Thendara* are as follows [13];

- Invoiced price £18,500
- Hull materials £7,253 and hull labour £5,848
- Overheads contribution £2,998, and net profit £2,401

To put these figures into context, the *Thendara* cost approached about half that of the £47,816 charged for the small motor ship *Karu* built around the same time (yard number 546) for the New Zealand Steam Ship Company. This vessel was much larger than *Thendara* at 1044 gross tons, 220ft long and 35ft beam, with an 810hp engine. Despite the approximately ten times greater size, the *Karu* hull labour cost of £9,158 was only twice as much as the £5,848 incurred for the *Thendara*. However, the *Karu* required £8,077 for other labour associated with the engine and other machinery outfitting, not needed on the yacht.

Thendara was of composite construction, planked with teak on steel frames, and was built with a 72hp Gleniffer DB6 diesel engine (now fitted with a 238hp Volvo). Main dimensions are as follows;

Length over spars	120 ft (36.6 m)
Length on Deck	105 ft (32 m)
Length Waterline	72 ft (21.9 m
Beam	20 ft (6.1 m)
Draft	12.2 ft (3.7 m)
Displacement	104.7 tonnes
Sail Area	5,194 ft² (482 m²)

She was and is a gaff rigged ketch. Even in 1936, this rig was somewhat old fashioned; many gaff racing yachts were converting to Bermudan rig at the time. This led other sailors to doubt her performance but *Thendara* quickly revealed herself to be a formidable racer, winning many contests. She won both her class and the overall prize at the Torbay Coronation Regatta of 1937, with Loch Broom men onboard.

During World War Two, *Thendara* served in the Royal Navy on the River Clyde and elsewhere. She is recorded as a Balloon Barrage Vessel, based at Methil on the Firth of Forth, probably to protect the naval base at Rosyth. Several other yachts were part of this flotilla, including the *Cariad*, together with fishing vessels such as the drifters *Heathery Brae* and *Vine*.

Some cruising and racing continued after the end of the war, but in 1950, while at Bénodet in Brittany on the *Thendara*, Sir Arthur Young died. The yacht was sold to pay the death duties, and thereafter she changed owner numerous times, spending much of her time in the Mediterranean between Greece and Italy. Like many other classic yachts in the second half of the 20th century, *Thendara* was neglected and allowed to deteriorate over the decades.

Fortunately, in 1991 she was moved back to the UK where Southampton Yacht Services had been commissioned by Mike Horsley to carry out a full restoration. In 1994 *Thendara* was re-launched and won the Gaff Rigged prize in the 1998 Atlantic Challenge. *Thendara* joined a fleet of historic sailing yachts in Antigua for the annual Classic Regatta in 2000, winning her class, and taking first place in the *Boat International* Concours d' Elegance.

She is one of last surviving large cruising yachts constructed before World War II and one of the best-preserved yachts of her period still sailing today. In 2007 and 2011 *Thendara* was advertised for sale at an asking price of 4.95 million Euros.

Above: THENDARA launch
day at Stephen yard, Linthouse,
1937 (Barclay Curle and
Charles Connell shipyards
on opposite bank)
(MARC TURNER PFM Pictures)

Right: THENDARA in the
Firth of Clyde 1938
(PHOTO © BEKEN)

THENDARA during the Palma Vela
Regatta, Majorca, Spain, April 2010
(Alamy)

INTERNATIONAL
REGATTA

MARKING THE

CORONATION
YEAR, 1937

Patron
H.R.H. The Duke of Kent

BRITANNIA

1893 — 1936

Programme
of Races

At
TORBAY AND DARTMOUTH
JUNE 19th to JULY 3rd

Far left: Race Programme
for Torbay Coronation
Regatta of 1937

Left: William Brown
Trophy won by
THENDARA

Centre: Silver medal
struck to commemorate
the Torbay Coronation
Regatta of 1937

Below: MY THENDARA
as SULARA
(GL WATSON)

Earlier *Thendaras*

Arthur Young had previously owned two other vessels named *Thendara*. The first was an auxiliary yawl built at Shoreham in 1901, originally named *Brada,* which he owned from 1923 into the 1930s. She was 72 feet long overall with 55 feet waterline length. Loch Broom MacKenzies crewed on this boat as well as the later *Thendara.*

The second was a motor yacht which he owned for a brief period in 1935 and 1936. This vessel was built by Camper & Nicholson in 1924 (originally named *Aloha*) and was 90ft long overall and 16ft beam with a Thames measurement of 94 tons. She had two Gardner diesel engines and was also auxiliary rigged as a schooner. When sold she was renamed *Sulara* and was still on the yacht register in 1975, based in the South of France.

Thendara is the name of a small resort town in the Adirondack hills of New York State in the USA.

Loch Broom Men

The *Thendara* of 1937 was active for only two years before the war brought leisure sailing to an end. Consequently, there are fewer than might be expected photographs of her Loch Broom crew.

Danie "Buie" MacKenzie was the Skipper of at least two of the *Thendaras,* and most of his crew were from the Lochside. In some years they were all from that area, as in the photograph showing five MacKenzies and a MacLennan.

Earlier THENDARA crew (L-R) Willie "Painter" MacKenzie, Jimmy "Ferry" MacKenzie, John "Nelson" Mackenzie, Jimmy "Cloudy" MacLeod, unknown, Jackie "Buie" MacKenzie, unknown, Alick MacKenzie (brother of Edward), Danie "Buie" MacKenzie (skipper)
(Ullapool Museum)

Left: THENDARA crew with Roderick "Nelson" MacKenzie on right
(Eric MacKenzie photo)

Right: A THENDARA crew from the Lochside - Left to Right; John "Poley" MacLennan, Jackie "Buie" MacKenzie, Willie James MacKenzie, Skipper Danie "Buie" MacKenzie, Alick (Ali Iain Mhor) MacKenzie and John "Onorach" MacKenzie
(photo courtesy Finlay "Buie" MacKenzie)

In the new *Thendara's* first year the Torbay Coronation Regatta took place from 19th June to 3rd July 1937. The successful yacht then cruised up the West Coast of Scotland, calling at Ullapool on 21st July. On this voyage without the owner the crew is reported to have purchased nets in Glasgow and fished for salmon on their way up the coast. There are believed to be photographs in Ullapool homes of 30lb fish caught on this trip.

Uldra

The Yacht

Uldra was a cruising cutter built by William Fife of Fairlie in 1905. This vessel replaced James Robertson Blackie's previous boat *Mirza* (also built by Fife in 1899), which had been sold to St Petersburg, Russia.

Uldra had a Thames measurement of 56 tons, an overall length of 64.5 feet and beam of 14.5 feet. After Blackie died in 1911 *Uldra* was put up for sale, and by 1913 she was in France.

The Owner – James Blackie

James Robertson Blackie (1854 – 1911) was a partner in the book publishing firm of Blackie and Son. Blackie and Son was a publishing house operating from Glasgow and London between 1890 and 1991. The firm initially published books sold by subscription, including religious texts and reference books. Later the focus moved to educational texts and children's books.

James Robertson Blackie joined the firm in 1877 and became a partner in 1881. His home was at Ferndean, Cove, on the Rosneath peninsula.

It appears that he paid for a headstone to be erected in Clachan churchyard, Loch Broom in memory of John MacKenzie, Skipper of the *Uldra* (died 1908).

James Robertson's cousin, Walter Wilfred Blackie (1860-1953), left the firm to live in Canada but was persuaded to return in 1884, becoming Chairman in 1918. He commissioned Charles Rennie MacIntosh to design the famous *Hill House* in Helensburgh in 1902.

Vadura

The Yacht

Vadura was a big gaff rigged auxiliary yawl of 111 tons Thames measurement, 104ft length over spars, 91.5ft on deck, 65ft on the water-line, with 19.3ft beam and 12.5ft draft. Her mainsail was 1,890 square feet in area, and her normal upwind sail area was more than 3,800 square feet.

She was built at the shipbuilding yard of Stephen of Linthouse, Glasgow to the design of Alfred Mylne (design number 298), using composite construction with steel frames and teak planking. Unusually, she also used heavy scantling teak for the stem, keel, sternpost and rudder, and had over 30 tons of lead in her keel, which was cast on the berth, in the yard. An engine of 30hp was installed. *Vadura* was ordered by Maurice Clark of the Paisley thread-making family and completed in May 1926.

Maurice Clark selected names beginning with the letter V for his yachts (e.g. *Vorsa*, *Vrona*). Vadura is the name of a village in the Swiss Alps, not far from Davos and Lichtenstein. The name is also similar to that of the 90ft steel yacht *Vanduara* built in Glasgow for John Clark in 1880. Vanduara is the old Roman name for a settlement near what is now Paisley.

Vadura (yard number 512) was ordered at Stephens at the same time as relative Kenneth Clark's order for the much larger and more expensive 230 ton motor yacht *Mingary* (yard number 511). Stephen recorded losses on both these orders. The figures recorded in the Stephen's records for *Vadura* are as follows [13];

- Invoiced price £12,629
- Hull materials £6,526 and hull labour £4,659, machinery £468
- Overheads contribution £3,849, and net loss £2,873

To put these figures into context, they are of the same order of magnitude as Stephen's project to build the oceangoing tug *Forceful* (yard number 509) for the Australasian Company at a price of £21,159. This vessel was much larger than *Vadura* at 288 gross tons, 115ft long and 27ft beam, with a 1000hp engine, but the hull labour cost of £3,722 was less than the £4,659 incurred for the *Vadura*. Of course, the tug required additional labour associated with the engine and other machinery outfitting, to the tune of £4,159.

In December 1940 *Vadura* was requisitioned by the Admiralty for use as a Harbour Defence Patrol Craft. She is listed in the Royal Navy Western Approaches Command, but is also recorded as based at Rosyth as a Balloon Barrage Vessel. When she was requisitioned *Vadura* had been laid up at the Morris & Lorimer yacht building yard at Sandbank in the Holy Loch, and when she fitted out with the barrage balloon handling gear, her masts, booms and gaffs were left stored in the yard's spar loft.

Maurice Clark died in 1941 and, after the war, the Howden family (another dynasty of Clydeside industrialists) spotted the hulk of *Vadura* at the Kyles of Bute. She was painted grey all over and moored to a large unprotected steel buoy, with a large chunk of her stem chewed away by the buoy [5]. James Howden Hume established where *Vadura*'s spars were stored and then made a successful bid to the Receiver of Wrecks for the yacht. He also managed to persuade the Board of James Howden & Co. to purchase the Morris & Lorimer yard, and their first job was to repair *Vadura*'s hull and bring her back up to her pre-war standard. Planks from the yard's pre-war store of long-seasoned boat-building teak were used for this work.

Archie Currie, a Tighnabruaich fisherman in the winter months, worked for the Howden Humes as *Vadura*'s professional skipper during the summer. In the Hume's time, the crew usually included four paid hands, including a cook, who looked after the yacht as if they owned it – every piece of brass was sparkling, the varnished wood impeccably bright and the teak decks scrubbed spotlessly white.

By the late 1960s, *Vadura* was owned by Gerard Leclery of Paris. Leclery was a millionaire French movie producer and actor, and onboard guests included Brigitte Bardot amongst others. *Vadura* adventured throughout the Mediterranean and the Pacific and was still in good condition and present off Fremantle when Australia hosted the America's Cup in 1987. By the 1990s she was in the USA and getting tired, and as of 2008 *Vadura* was in Sausalito, California, in urgent need of restoration. She was still afloat, but her interior was gutted and she had temporary plywood decks keeping the water out. There was reported to be a storage unit ashore full of her interior, deck hardware and sails.

Vadura's First Owner – Maurice Clark

Vadura first owner was James Henry Maurice Clark (1892-1941), a prominent and popular Glasgow businessman and yachtsman.

J H Maurice Clark was the son of Robert Clark of Troon. He was educated at Loretto School, Musselburgh, and Trinity College, Cambridge (engineering BA 1913, MA 1918). During the Great War, he served in the RNVR. In World War Two he again served in the RNVR as a Captain, but was retired medically unfit in July 1941 and died in September of that year.

VADURA on the Clyde in 1934
(photograph by GLA Blair of Paisley, FRPS)

A small lighthouse marking the eastern side of the Garvel Embankment at the Great Harbour of Greenock was renamed Maurice Clark Point in 1943, in recognition of his work as Commanding Officer of the Clyde Division of the RNVR.

Maurice Clark had interests in ship owning, operating the Clark & Service firm out of 21 Bothwell Street, Glasgow together with his father Robert, but he was also a director of the large Paisley cotton thread firm Clark & Co.

This business began in 1755 when James and Patrick Clark started a silk thread and loom equipment business in Paisley. In 1806 Patrick Clark invented a method of twisting cotton threads together to make a fine substitute for silk thread which had become unavailable due to the Napoleonic Wars. He opened the first factory for manufacturing cotton thread in 1812, and in 1864 the Clark family began production in Newark, New Jersey as the Clark Thread Co. These business connections in North America (source of the cotton raw material, and a large market for thread) continued over many years. From 1896 the Clark firm co-operated with its equally famous Paisley neighbour J&P Coats, eventually merging in the early 1950s.

Both the Clark and Coats families were heavily involved in yachting, with many members owning boats and placing repeat orders at builders like Fife of Fairlie. It is said that at one Clyde regatta after the First World War, no fewer than 20 vessels were flying either the Clark or Coats house flags.

J H Maurice Clark was a keen sailor of International 6-Metre class yachts, and was a vice-commodore of the Royal Northern Yacht Club (later RNCYC). He competed regularly in the USA as well as the UK, with his 6-Metre yachts *Vrana* and *Vorsa* among the top British contenders for the Seawanhaka Cup.

One Saturday morning during the 1930s, when returning from a business trip to the USA, this gentleman is reported to have jumped into the sea off the stern of a delayed transatlantic passenger ship entering the Clyde. He was picked up by the waiting family motor launch in order to make the start of a yacht race which would be missed if he had remained onboard while the liner proceeded up river to berth.

Clark Relatives

Maurice Clark was a nephew of George S Clark (1861 - 1935), who was a co-founder of the Workman Clark shipyard in Belfast (mentioned elsewhere in this chapter in connection with yachts *Morna* and *Hotspur*). George Clark was a son of James Clark of the thread mill family.

Other more famous but possibly less industrious members of this family included Kenneth Mackenzie Clark (1868–1932), his only child the art historian Kenneth Clark (1903 – 1983), and the latter's son Alan Clark (1928 – 1999), the politician and diarist.

J. H. M. CLARK.

TELEPHONE: CENTRAL 6782.
TELEGRAMS: CARE "CREVICE," GLASGOW.

21 BOTHWELL STREET,
GLASGOW. C.2.

26th. September, 1939.

TO WHOM IT MAY CONCERN.

This is to certify that Mr. J. A. McKenzie joined my auxiliary yawl "VADURA" as Deck Hand at the beginning of the season 1939 and served till the yacht was laid up, during which time he proved himself a capable and willing hand, being at all times strictly sober and attentive to his duties.

During the season he served as professional hand on my 6 metre yacht "VRANA", being his first experience in that position, and I found him very eager to learn the job. By the end of the season he was proficient in the work and kept the racing boat and her gear in excellent condition.

This reference is given in case any one can make use of his services during the present emergency, as I can thoroughly recommend him to anyone who can utilise his services about boats.

It is my intention to re-engage him as soon as possible after the present state of affairs is over and my boats are in commission again.

Reference for Jackie "Buie" MacKenzie written by Maurice Clark of VADURA, 1939
(courtesy Finlay "Buie" MacKenzie)

Main image: Anchor Mills, Paisley, 2015
(© User : Colin / Wikimedia Commons / CC BY-SA 4.0)

Loch Broom Men
Upper right: VADURA crew - John "Jock" MacKenzie (Loggie), Alec "Lally" MacKenzie, Alec
Macleod (Aultbea), John MacPherson
(Ullapool Museum)

Lower right: Lally (Alec MacKenzie) on VADURA
(Ullapool Museum)

Kenneth Mackenzie Clark (1868–1932) was briefly a director of the thread firm but retired in his mid-twenties to join the "idle rich". His son memorably claimed, "*although many people were richer, there can have been few who were idler*". He is believed to have been one of the men who "broke the bank" at Monte Carlo. The Clarks wintered on the French Riviera and maintained large country houses at Sudbourne Hall, Suffolk and Glenborrodale Castle, Ardnamurchan, from where Kenneth was an active member of the Western Isles Yacht Club at Tobermory. Clark entertained lavishly at Glenborrodale and also let it at various times to fellow yachting enthusiasts such as Sir Tom Sopwith and Sir Thomas Lipton. Amongst others, he ordered the Fife built *The Ketch* (1906), *Kentra* (1923), and the motor yacht *Mingary* (1926).

The art historian Kenneth Mackenzie Clark (1903 – 1983) was also a museum director, writer and broadcaster. During the 1950s and 1960s, he presented a succession of television programmes about the arts, culminating in the BBC series *Civilisation* in 1969.

The politician Alan Kenneth Mackenzie Clark (1928 – 1999) was a Conservative Member of Parliament, author and diarist. He served as a junior minister in Margaret Thatcher's governments and became a Privy Counsellor in 1991. Alan Clark became well known for his indiscretions, flamboyance and wit. His diary is a candid account of political life in Margaret Thatcher's Conservative Party.

Valentine

The Yacht

Valentine was a yacht owned during the 1920s by Andrew MacGeorge, who later commissioned the building of the *Roska*.

Originally called *Pavonia*, she was built at WG Luke on the Hamble in 1902. She was an auxiliary yawl, of 52ft length overall, 36'6" waterline length and 11ft beam. After *Roska* was built in 1930, *Valentine* was sold, and in 1937 was listed as owned by a Captain Stuart of Greenock.

Some of the Loch Broom crewmen moved from the *Valentine* to the *Roska*, including Skipper William "Black" MacKenzie.

Loch Broom Men and Women
Crew and visitors on VALENTINE, skipper W. MacKenzie in front
(Kate Rettie Photo)

Vida VI

The Yacht

Vida VI was designed and built by William Fife at Fairlie in 1906 (yard number 516). She was originally built as a gaff yawl, 73ft long, 60ft waterline length and 16'3" beam, with a Thames measurement of 80 tons.

First built without an engine, in 1920 a 2 cylinder Bergius paraffin motor was installed. By 1938 this was replaced by a more powerful 8 cylinder Chrysler petrol motor.

This yacht was originally built for a James Frame with offices at 106 Buchanan Street, Glasgow, and named *Rose*, a name she bore through several ownership changes. In 1920 William Wylie of Woodside Terrace, Glasgow is recorded by Lloyds as the owner, and in 1921 she is listed with her name changed to *Vida VI*.

Wylie is still listed as the owner in 1935, but by 1937 *Vida VI* had been sold twice and renamed *Thelma*. She was later known as *Griselda* when owned by Mr Oswald Graham of Hamilton. He continued to sail her on the Clyde and she remained on the river of her creation until 1970 or so. Later, she was engaged in charter work in the Caribbean as *Double Cross,* but her present whereabouts are not known.

The Owner – William Wylie

William Adam Wylie (1856 - 1939) owned the vessel for several years, and it may be his son who appears in the photograph below with the Loch Broom men. This family controlled the Glasgow cabinet making and interior outfitting firm of Wylie & Lochhead. William's home was at 13 Woodside Terrace in the West End of the city.

Wylie & Lochhead was founded in 1829 by cabinet-makers Robert Wylie and William Lochhead. This business flourished in 1832 as a result of high demand for coffins on account of a serious epidemic of cholera in Glasgow, undertaking then being an activity traditionally associated with cabinet-makers. Wylie & Lochhead took care of most of these funerals, as competitors were unwilling to risk handling the deceased. They later became successful producing high-quality furniture at their workshops in Glasgow. Wylie & Lochhead also opened showrooms in big cities like London and Manchester and began selling abroad in the USA. The firm became renowned for its use of modern artistic designs and high standards of craftsmanship.

By the 1870s, they were the first of the Glasgow furnishers to specialise in ship and yacht interiors, and worked as sub-contractors and suppliers for yachts built by Fife and others.

VIDA VI under sail
(Eric MacKenzie photo)

In the straitened economic climate after the First World War, Wylie & Lochhead introduced cheaper product lines, and during the Second World War they produced utility furniture. The department store chain House of Fraser acquired the stores of Wylie & Lochhead in 1957, though the firm continued to trade under its own name, focusing mainly on the funeral undertaker business.

William A Wylie was a keen yachtsman who had owned several previous small yachts named *Vida*, with which he was a successful racer around the turn of the century. These were the first *Vida* (1893), *Vida II* (1895) and *Vida III* (1901), all designed by GL Watson.

Buchanan Street, Glasgow, early 1930s – Wylie & Lochhead store on left (with bay windows)
(no publisher identified)

In about 1926, when aged 70, Wylie had a serious accident while mooring *Vida* at Cove on the north side of the Clyde. His foot caught in the anchor chain and was almost severed. He instructed the Skipper to tie a tourniquet, and they made for the hospital at Greenock on the south side of the Clyde where the foot was amputated.

Loch Broom Men

Many Lochside men worked on the *Vida VI*, including Danie "Buie" MacKenzie who was the skipper. Murdo MacLean (1865-1949) from Ardindrean and his son Murdo were among the crew.

Crew at bow of VIDA VI – Danie "Buie" MacKenzie 2nd from left
(Maymie MacKenzie photo)

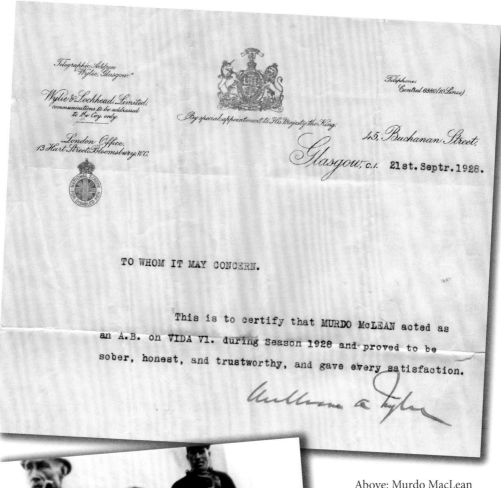

Telegraphic Address
"Wylie, Glasgow"

Wylie & Lochhead, Limited.
communications to be addressed
to the Coy. only.

London Office,
13 Hart Street, Bloomsbury, W.C.

By special appointment to His Majesty the King.

Telephones
Central 6880 (10 Lines)

45, Buchanan Street,
Glasgow, c.1. 21st. Septr. 1928.

TO WHOM IT MAY CONCERN.

This is to certify that MURDO McLEAN acted as
an A.B. on VIDA VI. during Season 1928 and proved to be
sober, honest, and trustworthy, and gave every satisfaction.

Above: Murdo MacLean
reference from William Wylie
for service on VIDA VI, 1928
(courtesy Ian & Murdo MacLean)

Left: Crew of yacht VIDA VI
with Mr Wylie's family. Back
right; John "Nelson" MacKenzie
(uncle of Eric MacKenzie),
2nd row left; Murdo MacLean
(father of Johnny & Murdo,
uncle of Angie "Allan"
MacKenzie), 2nd row centre;
Danie "Buie" MacKenzie
(Ullapool Museum)

Left: VIDA VI crew – Danie "Buie" MacKenzie 2nd from right
(Eric MacKenzie photo)

Right: VIDA VI crew gathered at the stern – Danie "Buie" MacKenzie at back left –
Note the steering tackles on the tiller
(Eric MacKenzie photo)

Waratah

The Yacht

This was a small wooden vessel of 19 tons Thames measurement and 42ft length. She was schooner rigged and built in 1877 at a specially established boatyard on the south side of Little Loch Broom (the boatbuilder is recorded as a MacKenzie). The name comes from a flowering shrub which grows in the owner's native south-east Australia.

Despite her small size, this boat apparently cruised in the North Sea, including to the coast of Norway. Following the death of her owner Murdo MacKenzie, she was sold to a Thomas Berry of Dundee in 1883.

The Owner – Murdo MacKenzie

Murdo Munro MacKenzie (1843 – 1881) was the laird of Dundonnell for a short period from 1878 until his death. He belonged to the Australian branch of the MacKenzie landlords and inherited the estate in 1878 on the death of his father Kenneth. Kenneth was born in Scotland in 1806 and returned to take possession of his late brother's estate in 1870. Murdo lived in Scotland before his father died and was fond of cruising around the Ross-shire coast.

Murdo died after he contracted pneumonia following a cold-water drenching onboard the *Waratah* off the coast of Norway. Apparently, the voyage was in winter, the boat was caught in a storm, and an inadequately dressed Murdo had come on deck to assist the crew.

Murdo had no legitimate heir, and on his death the Dundonnell estate (including Kildonan and Scoraig) passed to his brother Hugh (1845 - 1917) who preferred to remain in Australia.

Loch Broom Men

Gregor MacGregor of Scoraig was the Skipper of the *Waratah*. Other men from Little Loch Broom also sailed on her.

Zara

The Yacht

Zara was a large steam yacht designed by GL Watson and built by the Ailsa Shipbuilding Company of Troon in 1895. Her first owner was Peter Coats of the Paisley thread-making firm.

This *Zara* is not to be confused with the smaller (249 tons) *Zara* of 1891 which Peter Coats had built by Fleming & Ferguson in Paisley in 1891, and sold to the USA after taking delivery of the new yacht. This older *Zara* found her way into the US Navy in 1917 where she served as a patrol vessel on Long Island Sound.

ZARA of 1895
(GL WATSON)

The *Zara* of 1895 was 516 tons Thames measurement on a length of 178ft and beam of 25ft. During World War One *Zara* was hired by the Admiralty (Pendant No. 062) and fitted with two 3 inch guns. She was in service from March 1915 to March 1919 and may have served as wireless-equipped Auxiliary Patrol Group Leader at home or in the Mediterranean.

The Owner – Peter Coats

Peter Coats Junior (1842 - 1913), was the third son of Sir Peter Coats (1808 - 1890) whose father James had founded the huge Coats thread-making empire of Paisley, described in connection with the yacht *Gleniffer*. Peter Coats was a younger brother of Sir James Coats (1834 - 1913) and a cousin of *Gleniffer* owner James Coats Junior.

Like other members of the Coats family, Peter contributed generously to many local Paisley charities, including £10,000 towards the Royal Alexandra Infirmary and associated home for nurses in the late 1890s, and the addition of a wing to the local art gallery.

He was unmarried, and on his death in 1913 the *Zara* passed to his brother Daniel. After Daniel died in 1922, the yacht was bought by Bartow van Voorhis of Philadelphia, but then moved to Egypt before returning to Scotland in 1926.

Loch Broom Men

Kenneth MacRae (1862 - 1926) was on *Zara* when war broke out in August 1914 and did not pay off till October 1914. Other Lochside men were also employed on her.

THE MEN AND
THEIR FAMILIES

The Lochside Communities

Most of the Loch Broom area men who worked on the yachts came from the south side of upper Loch Broom, known locally as the Lochside. Going west along the steep north-facing slopes of the loch are small communities named Letters, Ardindrean, Rhiroy, Blarnalearach and Loggie.

The flat farming land around Clachan at the head of Loch Broom has been attractive real estate for many centuries, but the steep hills further west were mainly settled in the mid-1800s by families who were evicted from Dundonnell, Kildonan, Scoraig and Inverlael.

In particular, the "Allan" Mackenzie family came to Letters around 1839, from the Dundonnell area over the hill to the south, while the "Buie" family of MacKenzies came from Inverlael on the north side of the loch.

The crofts in Letters were owned by the Church of Scotland and the crofters paid a nominal rent to the Church. The crofts and ground west from the school at Ardindrean to Rhiroy and Loggie were and are still owned by Dundonnell Estate.

The displaced people made their living as best they could from both land and sea, with the small crofting acreage unable on its own to support the large families of the time. The steep hills made cultivation difficult ("*you needed a ladder to plant the potatoes*"), although it was said that this made the men well adapted to working on the heeled deck of a sailing yacht !

A photograph of the Lochside taken in the 1930s shows the land well cultivated on every croft. Owing to the steepness of the land, the ground was often turned by the old fashioned *cas chrom* foot plough into the 20th century. Fertiliser was mainly seaweed and cow dung. The seaweed was gathered at low tide from the shallow areas at the head of Loch Broom and brought back by boat. Hard labour was then required to carry it up the hill in creels on the backs of the people. The seaweed produced high-quality vegetables and potatoes. Hay and corn were also grown to feed livestock. One or two cows were owned by each crofter, and butter and cheese were made by every home.

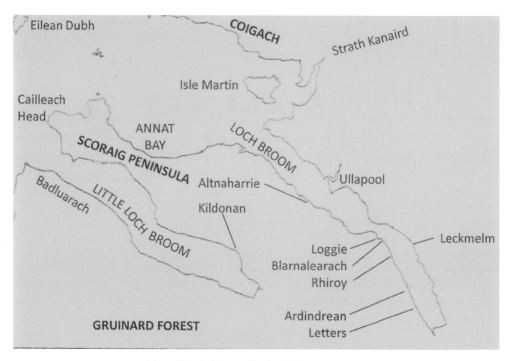

Map of Loch Broom "lochside" communities

Well cultivated crofts on Lochside – first half of 20th century –
view south from the Garve Road on north side of Loch Broom
(JB White postcard)

Left: Steep Lochside hills from the NW in 2008
(cc-by-sa/2.0 - © Ike Gibson - geograph.org.uk/p/1108277)

Right: Ploughing the steep slopes at Letters, 1950 – Duncan "Tor" MacKenzie, son of John "Onorach"
(Ullapool Museum)

A road was not built to the Lochside until the 1930s, and this circumstance kept the population closely connected with the sea well into the 20th century.

There was a small shop at Ardindrean, but people regularly rowed or sailed to Ullapool for supplies. For larger purchases, people made use of catalogue shopping. Until the 1920s, floating shops also-called from time to time, and the residents rowed out to the ship to make their purchases.

Collecting the mail at Ardcharnich – Hugh MacKenzie at bow, Sandy "Buie" MacKenzie at oars
(Ullapool Museum)

The Loch Broom Men

For the yacht owners, the West Highland men represented a very attractive labour force. They had grown up with the sea and boats and had a reputation for honesty and hard work. Experience on a range of different types of sailing fishing vessels equipped the Loch Broom men with the skills and strength needed to work on yachts. In addition, the native West Highland discretion and diplomacy were likely to be useful virtues on a yacht. Also, their wage demands were no doubt acceptably low.

West Coast men had earned a living from the sea for generations, often as self-employed fishermen in small boats in their home waters, or as hired crew on larger East Coast vessels. There was a long tradition of men from the West Coast and the Western Isles travelling (often by foot) to the East coast ports such Helmsdale and Wick to obtain seasonal employment on the huge fleets of herring drifters working there. Women-folk would also make the long trek to work in gutting teams. From the 1840s or earlier, Lochbroom boat owners were making the dangerous voyage to the east coast herring fishery in their own small un-decked vessels.

In the later decades of the 19th century earnings from this work allowed some Wester Ross men to purchase larger boats more suited to following the North Isles and East Coast fisheries. Most of these were probably luggers of the Scaffie type, sold on by Moray Firth owners after the introduction of the Zulu.

Around the turn of the 20th century, the Loch Fyne Skiff type of boat became popular in the North West Highlands. This was a boat with a single standing lugsail, usually around 30 feet in length, but sometimes larger. They had a small forecastle in which four or five men could sleep, and this allowed crews to fish all over the Minch, and sometimes down to the Clyde. In the North West, motors did not start to be fitted to these vessels until after 1910 or so.

In the last 20 years of the 19th century, the sailing herring drifters reached large dimensions, with Fifies and Zulus of 70ft and 80ft length being common. Such vessels continued to be built until about 1904, and although their decline after that was rapid, several continued to sail for decades thereafter. Stornoway had 130 sailing fishing vessels in 1906, 24 in 1923 and only four in 1936.

The gear and sails on these big luggers were heavy and of similar dimensions to the sails carried by quite substantial racing yachts. For example, a big Zulu would have a foresail area of 1,600 ft², a mizzen of 1,300 ft² and occasionally set an 800 ft² jib. This total area of 3,700 ft² approaches the 3,800 ft² of a 90 feet cruiser such as *Vadura* or the 4,500 ft² of a heavily canvassed 15-Metre racer.

Although spars on the fishing luggers were not as long as the 90 foot booms on the biggest racing yachts, they were still heavy, and had to be handled by much smaller crews in all weathers and at night. A herring drifter foresail yard might be about 36 feet long, while the jib boom would be about 52 feet long and run out and inboard at sea. Equally difficult was the lowering and raising of the 3 tonne foremast at sea, an operation which was usually performed every night to help the drifter ride to her fleet of drift nets.

The lug sails of these boats were set to one side of the mast and were more dangerous and difficult to handle than the pure fore and aft rigs of the yachts. Although the big herring luggers had crews of seven or eight when fishing, they frequently had to make passage with smaller crews of only three or four. For example, in November 1897 when coming home from the East Anglian herring fishing. the big Stornoway Zulu *Caberfeidh* SY1108 (Alex MacLeod, 1866 - 1954) landed three East coast crew members in Aberdeen and proceeded towards the Pentland Firth with a reduced complement of four. There, they met heavy weather and the foresail yard broke, injuring one of the crew, but the three fit men were able to bring the damaged *Caberfeidh* safely to Lewis.

With this type of experience, summer season work on the sailing yachts would not have presented any difficulties to West Highland fishermen.

It is not known how the men from the Loch Broom area were first offered work on yachts but it is possible that local landlords provided the first employment for Loch Broom crews. The MacKenzie lairds of Dundonnell and John Fowler of Braemore were yacht owners before 1880. Later, Pirie and Calvert of Leckmelm were employers of local sailors.

The 1881 census records the occupation of Alexander MacKenzie from Letters as "*Captain of Yacht*". By 1891 there were at least 13 men from the area crewing on yachts, and the numbers continued to grow, reaching 22 in 1901. The census was taken in the spring, and therefore the records do not account for those who may have been away from home at that time.

The Lochside was a close-knit community with many family interconnections. Extended family members often crewed together on the same boat. Once one man had secured a berth, he would be able to assist other relations to join the crew. For example, the "Buie" MacKenzie family were strongly represented on both of Arthur Young's *Thendara* yachts during the 1930s. From the letters and photographs, it also seems that Skipper Danie "Buie" MacKenzie moved from the *Vida VI* to the *Thendara*, together with most of his crew. Sisters of Danie "Buie" married Lochside men who also found work on the yachts.

The "Allan" MacKenzies are found as "yachtsmen" in the census from 1891 onwards. In the early 20th century Allan MacKenzie (Allan Mor) served as cook/steward on several yachts including the *Jeano*. Allan Mor had several MacRae forebears sailing on various yachts including the *Oceana*. His Uncle Kenneth MacRae sailed as far as the Baltic on the beautiful Coats schooner *Gleniffer*. Allan Mor's son "Angie Allan" was one of the last Lochside men to find employment on the yachts, working on them until 1950.

The employment opportunities on British yachts began to decline as a result of the First World War, and virtually vanished after the Second World War. In the 1950s only two or three men from the Lochside were employed as yacht crew.

ON THE YACHTS

1891 Census (5th April) – Lochside Yachtsmen/Sailors

Name	Age	Occupation	Community
John MacKenzie	48	Ship Captain	Letters
Duncan McRae	33	Yachtsman	Letters
John McRae	30	Yachtsman	Letters
Murdo McDonald	23	Sailor	Letters
James McKenzie	28	Sailor	Letters
John McLeay	28	Sailor	Letters
Alexander McKenzie	30	Sailor	Letters
Murdo McLean	26	Sailor	Letters
Kenneth MacNab	24	Sailor	Ardindrean
Kenneth McKenzie	25	Sailor	Blarnalearach
John McKenzie	22	Sailor	Blarnalearach
Roderick McKenzie	20	Sailor	Blarnalearach
Alexander McRae	24	Sailor	Blarnalearach

1901 Census (31st March) – Lochside Yachtsmen/Sailors

Name	Age	Occupation	Community
John McKenzie	59	Captain of yacht	Letters
Alexander McKenzie	23	Yachtsman	Letters
Murdo McKenzie	21	Yachtsman	Letters
John McRae	41	Yachtsman	Letters
Kenneth McRae	38	Yachtsman	Letters
Roderick McKenzie	22	Yachtsman	Letters
Kenneth McDonald	37	Yachtsman	Letters
John McLeay	37	Yachtsman	Letters
James McKenzie	38	Yachtsman	Letters
John Munro	21	Yachtsman	Letters
Murdo McLean	36	Yachtsman	Letters
Donald Rose	41	Yachtsman	Letters
Duncan Rose	31	Yachtsman	Letters
John McLeod	37	Yachtsman	Letters
Alexander McLeod	33	Yachtsman	Letters
Donald McKenzie	19	Yachtsman	Letters
Alexander McLennan	17	Yachtsman	Letters

*1901 Census (31st March) – Lochside Yachtsmen/Sailors (**cont.**)*

Name	Age	Occupation	Community
John McLennan	15	Yachtsman	Letters
John McKenzie	29	Yachtsman	Ardindrean
Donald McLeod	18	Yachtsman	Ardindrean
Kenneth McKenzie	33	Yachtsman	Blarnalearach
Roderick McKenzie	30	Yachtsman	Blarnalearach

1911 Census (2nd April) – Lochside Yachtsmen/Sailors

Name	Age	Occupation	Community
Edward McKenzie	19	Yachtsman & Fisher	Letters
John McKenzie	25	Sailor	Letters
Alick McKenzie	24	Sailor	Letters
Alick MacNab	24	Sailor	Letters
John McLeay	55	Yachtsman	Letters
Alick McLeay	21	Yachtsman	Letters
Dan/Donald McLeay	19	Yachtsman	Letters
Kenneth McLeay	17	Yachtsman	Letters
Murdo McDonald	22	Sailor	Letters
James McKenzie	48	Seaman	Letters
Simon McKenzie	23	Seaman	Letters
James McKenzie	20	Seaman	Letters
John McKenzie	17	Seaman	Letters
Allan MacKenzie	23	Seaman	Letters
Simon MacKenzie	18	Seaman	Letters
Murdo McLean	45	Yachtsman & Fisher	Letters
John Munro	31	Sailor	Letters
Roderick Munro	22	Sailor	Letters
John McKenzie	39	Yachtsman & Fisher	Ardindrean
William McKenzie	37	Yachtsman & Fisher	Ardindrean
Duncan McLeod	31	Seaman	Ardindrean
Donald McLeod	28	Seaman	Ardindrean
William Munro	26	Sailor	Rhiroy
Alick McLennan	28	Sailor (acting AB)	Loggie

Skiff XL (UL 111) of
the Loch Fyne type, at
Scoraig in the 1920s
(MacGregor photo)

Zulu herring lugger with
foresail partly lowered
(courtesy Scottish
Fisheries Museum)

Life on the Yachts

The regular and predictable hard cash income was the main attraction for men coming from what was still basically a subsistence and barter economy, with few options for local waged employment. The living and working conditions onboard would be more congenial than those to be found on a fishing boat or coasting vessel.

For the Highland seamen, the yachting season also fitted in better with the cycle of the crofting year than deep sea merchant shipping. They could usually do the spring work such as cutting the peats and sowing the crops before departing for the south. On their return in September they would usually be in time to take in the harvest and the peats.

The Lochside men would often travel south together in large groups at the start of the season. MacBrayne's steamers connected Loch Broom and other small West Highland communities with Glasgow, but most men would cross Loch Broom in the family boat to catch the Ullapool to Garve mail bus (packed with other yachtsmen). From Garve railway station, the train would take them on to Inverness and the long journey down to Glasgow to meet up with other crew members and the owners of the yachts.

When away, the men usually wrote home weekly, enclosing a proportion of their pay. Murdo MacLennan remembers his father John sent home £1 per week.

On the cruising yachts, much of the activity took place at the weekends. The Clyde owners would usually join their boats at Gourock on a Friday evening, and the yachts would sail from

Garve Mail Bus at Ullapool, 1920s
(© Scottish Motor Museum Trust)

Group on MacBrayne's
steamer LOCHBROOM
which served the NW
coast in the 1930s
(Ullapool Museum)

their bases at Hunter's Quay, Sandbank or Dunoon in the afternoon to meet them there. A small flotilla of yacht tenders would be waiting for the owners to arrive in Port Glasgow or Greenock by car or train.

Sometimes the extended cruises of the yachts would take them up the West Coast, and a stop off in Loch Broom was not uncommon. This would sometimes allow the men to spend a night or two at home during the season.

While away from home, there would often be the chance for the men to catch up from time to time with their many friends and relatives who had moved to Glasgow and the other industrial towns of west central Scotland, or were working on other yachts.

The work gave the opportunity to meet people from an entirely different social and educational background, although naturally some of the owners were less friendly and approachable than others. Probably the ability of the men to communicate in Gaelic allowed them to vent some of their inevitable frustrations without attracting the displeasure of their English speaking employers.

Life on the Lochside without the Men

The men would usually depart for the yachts in the spring, when the ploughing and planting of oats and potatoes was complete. In late spring the peats were also cut and left to dry. In order to complete the work in time to get away for the yachting season at the end of March or early April, the planting would sometimes take place with the ground covered in snow. The men's return would hopefully coincide with the harvest work.

The burden of keeping the croft going fell upon the women and family members left behind. The women and men who did not "go to the yachts" would continue with the regular tasks.

Cows required to be milked and sheep needed to be cared for, including clipped. Inshore fishing continued, and later in the season it would be time for cutting the hay, harvesting the oats, and lifting the potatoes.

Sometimes the yacht owners would ask for the men early and keep them later in the season. Those at home would then often require the help of neighbours to ensure that all the necessary work was done.

Lochside group with yachting jerseys in evidence, children including Kenny & Isabel Munro, Rhiroy
(Ullapool Museum)

Lochside children bringing home the harvest
(Ullapool Museum)

The shop (left) at Ardindrean, Loch Broom operated by Donald & Mary MacIver until 1958
(MacGregor photo)

MacGregors

Gregor MacGregor (*Waratah*)

Gregor MacGregor (1830 - 1904) was from Carnoch, Scoraig on Little Loch Broom. The MacGregors came to Scoraig from Torridon about 1800. Gregor skippered the laird of Dundonnell's little yacht *Waratah* in the late 1870s. This laird was the Australian born Murdo MacKenzie (1843-1881). Gregor may also have captained an earlier yacht named *Dodo* belonging to a previous owner of the Dundonnell estate (Murdo, laird from 1845-1869). The forebears of these MacKenzies were responsible for clearing many families from Kildonan and Dundonnell to Scoraig and elsewhere in 1840 and before.

Gregor MacGregor
(MacGregor photo)

Gregor MacGregor married Ann MacLeod in 1866, and they had six daughters and two sons, including Roderick MacGregor (1870 - 1941), father of William MacGregor who later crewed on the *Roska*.

The other son was Duncan "Bar" MacGregor (1885 – 1961) who married Mary Munro in 1924. They lived at *Dal na Mara* on Shore Street, Ullapool. Mary died in 1991. They had no children.

The eldest daughter was Margaret (Peggy), born in 1866. She married Murdoch Campbell in 1882 and had six children, including Hector Campbell (1898 - 1975) who left Scoraig in 1962 with his family of Marie, Murdina and John Norman and lived at Pulteney Street, Ullapool.

The second daughter was Catherine (1868 - 1940). She married Donald MacRae and had eight children. One of these was Gregor MacRae (1897 - 1974) who married Mary MacKenzie and whose son was Billy MacRae (1934 – 2008). Gregor and family moved from Scoraig to Ullapool in the 1960s, where Billy commenced prawn fishing. Several of Billy MacRae's descendants live around Ullapool.

William MacGregor (*Roska*)

William MacGregor (1912 - 1973) was the son of Roderick MacGregor and Maxwell Allan Rae from Carnoch, Scoraig. He had two older brothers Robert Gordon and Gregor. William served three seasons on the *Roska* from 1937 to 1939, obtaining his last letter of reference from the owner on Monday 18th September 1939 (war was declared on Sunday 3rd September) – finding him to be, *"in every way satisfactory, willing and thoroughly honest"*. This was the same date and language as the reference provided to John MacLean (Johnny Clane).

Unlike most of the other men in this book, William MacGregor was not from the Lochside of the big Loch Broom. It is not known how he obtained his employment on the *Roska*, but it most likely was through contacts with the Lochside men.

After World War Two he married Alice MacIver of Scoraig, and they moved to Ullapool in the early 1960s via Badralloch and Altnaharrie. They had four sons (Roy, Alistair, James and

Upper left: William MacGregor at 4 Carnoch, Scoraig in 1948 – the croft tenancy was being given up – wearing a ROSKA jersey and jacket
(© Newsquest (Herald & Times))

Lower left: William MacGregor at Scoraig wearing ROSKA jersey
(MacGregor photo)

Below: William MacGregor on ROSKA
(MacGregor photo)

Gordon). Roy MacGregor lives in Ullapool and has made his living from the sea since he and his father were involved in the start of prawn fishing from Ullapool in the late 1960s/early 1970s with the old Zulu boat *Seaflower* and the Summers yole *Harvest Lily* (UL 32).

"Allan" MacKenzies

Family Overview

This MacKenzie family, as with other families on the Lochside, moved to the area during the Highland Clearances. They can be traced back to the Little Loch Broom area; Achneigie and Keppoch in particular, and came to Letters via Kildonan and Scoraig.

Allan MacKenzie, grandfather of Allan (Mor), and his family arrived in the 1830s, living on the shore at Letters. In 1866 he was jailed in Dingwall, along with two other Lochsiders, for tearing up eviction papers to have them removed from the land. In 1883, when he was 78, Allan is recorded as giving evidence to the Napier Commission. As well as the Christian name Allan, the family has carried the byname Allan for many generations.

Allan "Mor" MacKenzie (*Jeano*, *Sheila*, others)

Allan MacKenzie (1887 - 1965) was the grandson of the above mentioned Allan, and the son of Murdo MacKenzie and Margaret MacRae from Letters. Murdo and Margaret had four other

Murdo & Margaret "Allan" MacKenzie with their daughter Alexina at Burnbrae
(Photo courtesy Tania Hutchison)

children Johan, Alexina, Simon and Ann. When Allan was young they lived on the shore at *Millburn*, but later moved up the hill to *Burnbrae*.

His brother Simon also worked on the yachts before the war, but joined up in 1914, later transferring to the Tank Corps. After surviving nearly four years, he was killed on 23rd August 1918 during the offensive that brought World War One to an end.

Allan "Mor" worked on the yachts along with Simon from the early 1900s. He is known to have crewed on the *Jeano* and the *Sheila*, mostly as the cook. He was on the racing yacht *Jeano* with Kenny "Buie" MacKenzie when they were photographed together in 1913.

Allan "Mor" MacKenzie, while serving on JEANO, 1913
(Ullapool Museum)

Allan married Christina MacAulay from Lewis who he met in Glasgow. They had five children; Murdo Simon, Nancy, Iain, Danny and Angus ("Angie Allan"). Son Murdo Simon (died 1983, aged 59) was named after the lost brother, which is why that branch of the "Allan" MacKenzies is referred to as Simon and not Allan.

Descendants of Allan "Mor" still live in the Ullapool area, including son Angie "Allan" (below). Of Allan's other children, Danny's daughter Christine, Murdo's children Effie, Gordon and

Far left: Allan "Mor" MacKenzie
(Eric MacKenzie photo)

Left: Alec "Lally" MacKenzie (L) & Allan "Mor" MacKenzie
(Ullapool Museum)

Donald, and some grandchildren and great-grandchildren still stay in the area. Murdo's oldest son, Captain Murdo Allan MacKenzie (d. 2012), continued the seafaring life of his ancestors by spending thirty years in the Merchant Navy with Bank Line. Later he was Harbour Master at Ullapool.

Angus "Allan" Mackenzie (*Fiumara, Carraig*)

Angus MacKenzie (Angie Allan) was born at Letters in 1929, the son of Allan "Mor" above.

Angie spent time on William Wordie's *Fiumara* after World War Two. He took over on the *Fiumara* from an Ullapool man Duncan Campbell (uncle of Heather Cumming), who had moved to Glasgow for work. Angie was a sixteen-year-old deckhand on the *Fiumara* when she beat *Thendara* in the first post-war race from Hunters Quay to Tarbert, Loch Fyne in 1946. This was a great achievement as the larger *Thendara*'s owner and men had been boasting that she was unbeatable. Angie recalls *Fiumara* was moored up with all sails stowed, and the crew was sharing a bottle with Col. Wordie by the time *Thendara* crossed the line.

Angie "Allan" MacKenzie
(Ullapool Museum)

In 1949 Angie Allan joined James Lithgow's steam yacht *Carraig* and sailed as Mate before coming ashore to get married in about 1950. Angie ran the paper shop, ironmongers and draper's shop in Ullapool during the 1960s and 70s, as well as the sea angling boat *Gannet*. He owned his own motor yacht *Silvander* for seventeen years and was Rear Commodore of the Royal Highland Yacht Club.

Angie also had ironmongers shops in Gairloch and Inverness and moved there after his wife Ivy died in 1975. In 1996 he remarried and moved to the USA with his second wife Pamela Belyea. They have since returned to Ullapool, where they now live at *Fyffe House*, Pulteney Street. Angie's daughter Heather and grandsons Jamie and Matthew also live in Ullapool.

"Buie" MacKenzies

Family Overview

Like many other Lochsiders, these MacKenzies arrived there as a result of the Clearances, with this family coming from Inverlael. Roderick "Buie" MacKenzie (1837 – 1912) married Margaret (Peggy) MacLeod (1850 – 1925), the aunt of James "Cloudy" MacLeod (described later in this chapter).

Roderick is listed on the 1901 census as a fisherman and crofter. Margaret MacLeod's sister Ann married Finlay "Buie" MacKenzie. Finlay MacKenzie was a prominent Lochbroom fisherman and owned a big First Class fishing boat in 1908.

Roderick's father, John MacKenzie (1777-1868) was the first to be nicknamed "Buie". About 1800, he was press-ganged into the Royal Navy. During his service, which included the Battle of Trafalgar, he had a bad bout of jaundice or scurvy and became known by his Gaelic speaking shipmates as "An Buidhe" (the yellow one).

Roderick and Peggy's children were; John (b. 1875), Margaret, Isabella, Donald/Danie (b. 1882), Catherine, Alexander, Annie, Robina, Kenneth (b. 1892) and Christina (Teenie).

Brothers John, Dan and Kenneth sailed on the yachts before the First and Second World Wars. John's sons Roddy and Jackie also worked on the yachts between the wars. Robina and Teenie's husbands, John MacKenzie (Onorach) and Duncan MacKenzie (Bain), both sailed on the yachts.

Danie "Buie" MacKenzie (*Oceana, Vida VI, Thendara* and others)

Donald MacKenzie (1882 – 1946) was born at *Caberfeidh*, Letters and latterly lived at *Tighnabruaich*, Letters (the house is now called *Mo Dhachaidh*). He was the son of Roderick and Margaret MacKenzie and a brother of John and Kenny "Buie" below. Although christened Donald, like many other Highlanders of that name he was known as Dan or Danie (there is no Y in the Gaelic alphabet).

He married Jessie Munro (1886 – 1962) who was the sister of brother John's wife, Isabella Munro. They had no issue. Danie's funeral in June 1946 caused a one week delay in the wedding of his nephew, Jackie "Buie".

Danie worked on the *Oceana* in the 1920s and skippered the *Vida VI*. He seems to have moved to Arthur Young and the *Thendara* after William Wylie let go of the *Vida VI* in 1935. Many other Lochsiders found employment working for him. Danie appears in many of the group photographs in this book.

Kenny "Buie" MacKenzie (*Jeano*)

Kenny "Buie" MacKenzie (1892 - 1969) was from *Caberfeidh*, Letters, and latterly lived in Ullapool. He was the youngest son of Roderick and Margaret MacKenzie, and a brother of yachtsmen Danie/Donald (above) and John (below). Before 1914 Kenny sailed on the 15-Metre racing yacht *Jeano* along with Allan "Mor" MacKenzie (described elsewhere).

During World War One Kenny served in the Royal Navy, surviving the battle of Jutland and several other close brushes with death. He was awarded the DSM, and also the Russian Order

YACHT "THENDARA".

Sandbank
Oct; 20th 1937

This is to certify that the bearer
John. A. MacKenzie has been with me
in M. Y. "Thendara" as deck hand for two
seasons from April till October 1935.
and 1936. and in the sailing yacht "Thendara"
as A. B. from March till October 1937.
during that time he has given the
utmost satisfaction. being strictly
sober, willing, and obliging, and
a good seaman
I can highly recommend him to
anyone requiring his services

Signed
Daniel MacKenzie
Master

Upper left: Large yacht (possibly OCEANA) - Danie "Buie" MacKenzie
on rail at right, Roderick "Nelson" MacKenzie on deck
(Eric MacKenzie photo)

Upper right: Large steam yacht crew - Danie "Buie" MacKenzie left,
standing, Roderick "Nelson" MacKenzie right, standing
(Eric MacKenzie photo)

Above: Reference written for Jackie "Buie" Mackenzie written by Danie "Buie" Mackenzie, 1937
(courtesy Finlay "Buie" MacKenzie)

Left: Crew of a large yacht (possibly OCEANA) - Danie "Buie" MacKenzie on rail right
(Eric MacKenzie photo)

Right: Kenny "Buie" MacKenzie, 1913
(Ullapool Museum)

Kenny "Buie" MacKenzie
(left) in WW1
(Ullapool Museum)

of St. Ann for conspicuous bravery in saving his ship in the White Sea when an outbreak of fire in the vicinity of the ammunition magazine threatened the destruction of the vessel.

He married Dora MacLean (1899 - 1983) of Ullapool, whose father John (1864 - 1932) owned the grocery shop on Shore Street where *The Frigate* now is. On John MacLean's death Kenny took over this shop, and also ran the ironmongers shop at the Quay St corner now occupied by *Loch Broom Hardware*. This hardware shop provided an essential service to the people from the remote communities around Loch Broom. Kenny "Buie" understood their needs very well and stocked the types of tools and merchandise they required. He was generous in extending credit to local families in times of need.

His children were John MacKenzie (1933 - 2009), Mary Catherine Mackenzie (1928 - 2013), of *Weybank*, Mill Street, Ullapool and Peggy Lavelle (d. 2017). John became a Master Mariner with the Bank Line and was their representative in New Guinea and New Britain in the 1970s and 1980s before retiring to Ullapool. He is mentioned in travel writer Gavin Young's *Slow Boats Home*. Mary Catherine was a leading figure in Ullapool community affairs for many decades. Grandchildren and great-grandchildren of Kenny "Buie" still live in Ullapool, including grandson John Lavelle and his son Sean.

Kenny "Buie" MacKenzie's shop, Shore Street, Ullapool
(Ullapool Museum)

John "Buie" MacKenzie (*Uldra*, *Thendara* and others)

John "Buie" MacKenzie (1875 - 1955) was the eldest son of Roderick and Margaret MacKenzie, and the brother of Danie (Donald), Kenny "Buie" and others. He lived and died at *Caberfeidh*, Letters. John married Isabella Munro (1878-1930), the daughter of John and Isabella Munro, Rhiroy. They had two sons; Roderick (b. 1917) and Jackie (b. 1918). The boys were cousins of John, Mary Catherine and Peggy, whose father was Kenny "Buie".

John sailed on Arthur Young's yacht *Thendara*, and his sons also worked on the yachts before World War Two.

In the photograph below, John is pictured with other yacht crew and a catch of fine salmon. The story behind the salmon is unfortunately lost, but the gentleman on the right resembles a brother of Nurse Bella MacKenzie (1888-1977) whose father had the Ardindrean shop until the 1920s. The photograph may therefore have been taken in Lochbroom. It is unlikely that the yacht owner was aware of this use of his boat as a fishing vessel.

Above: A young John MacKenzie
(centre right with ULDRA jersey)

Right: John "Buie" MacKenzie on left and
Roddy "Nelson" MacKenzie sitting
Photo taken on the Clyde
(Eric MacKenzie photo)

Above: John "Buie" MacKenzie
(Ullapool Museum)

Left: John "Buie" MacKenzie
(Ullapool Museum)

Below: John's sons Roddy & Jackie "Buie" MacKenzie in the 1920s,
with Finlay "Buie" MacKenzie in background
(Ullapool Museum)

Roddy & Jackie (sons of John "Buie") front left – Finlay "Buie" MacKenzie in THENDARA jersey
(Ullapool Museum)

Roderick "Buie" MacKenzie (*Roska*)

Roddy "Buie" MacKenzie (1917 – 1942) was the son of John and Isabella MacKenzie above, and brother of Jackie below. He was born at *Caberfeidh*, Letters and named after his grandfather Roderick "Buie". In his yachting days before World War Two he sailed on the *Roska* and possibly the *Thendara*.

Roddy was 25 years old and engaged to be married when he lost his life on Friday, 4th September 1942, together with several other men from the Ullapool and Gairloch area who were onboard the naval tug *Romsey*. She was run down and sunk in the Clyde by the Northern Ireland mail steamer and most of her crew of 20 were lost.

The *Romsey* was built by Ferguson Bros, Port Glasgow in 1930 for service at Southampton port. In 1941 she was sent to Loch Ewe to act as a standby/rescue tug at the naval base. Her south coast crew did not fancy life in the north and were mostly replaced by local men. About August 1942 *Romsey* was ordered south to the Clyde where she was based at the old Admiralty Pier in Cardwell Bay near Gourock on the Clyde.

On the night of the collision the tug had been lying off Gourock Pier, but it appears that strong winds caused her to drag her anchor out into the shipping channel. War-time blackout regulations meant she was difficult to see and she was struck just before midnight by the *Lairdsburn* on

Far left: Roddy
"Buie" MacKenzie
on ROSKA
(MacGregor photo)

Left: Roddy "Buie"
MacKenzie (left)
on ROSKA with
William MacGregor
(MacGregor photo)

passage from Glasgow to Belfast. The *Romsey* sank in minutes with only four survivors. Many of the Wester Ross men could not swim. The vessel was salvaged a month later and the missing bodies recovered. Three of the men could not be identified and their families decided to bury them together in Gourock Cemetery. One of those was Roddy "Buie". There is no headstone, but a shrub was planted to mark Lair number 40 in Section F.

As for the *Romsey;* she was repaired and put back into service. After the war, the tug was returned to her owners and continued working until broken up in 1962.

Jackie "Buie" MacKenzie (*Thendara, Vadura*)

John or Jackie "Buie" MacKenzie (1918 - 1973) was the son of John and Isabella MacKenzie above, and brother of Roddy (also above). Jackie was born at *Caberfeidh*, Letters, and lived there all his life. Among the yachts he sailed on were the *Thendara* and the *Vadura*.

During World War Two Jackie served on the rescue tugs on the Clyde. There he met Gourock girl Jean (known as Sheana) McGeachan who he married on 12th June 1946. The wedding was delayed for one week because of the funeral of his uncle Danie "Buie" on 1st June. Jackie and Jean had four children; Isobel (died 1954, aged 6), Roddy, Jean (married name Adam) and Finlay. When Jackie died in 1973, his wife and Finlay moved back to Greenock. Finlay still lives in Greenock but holidays regularly on the Lochside.

Jackie "Buie" MacKenzie in
THENDARA jersey (L) with John
"Nelson" MacKenzie (R)
(Jean Adam photo, Ullapool Museum)

"Bain" MacKenzies

Duncan "Bain" Mackenzie (*Mafalda, Thendara*)

Duncan (1886 - 1978) was the son of William and Johanna MacKenzie, Ardindrean, who were married in 1875. William was a fisherman.

William's father John MacKenzie (Buie) and Johan's father Colin MacKenzie (Bain) had both come to the Lochside after being evicted from Inverlael in 1819. They stayed with their wives and families at Crooked Bridge, Clachan, in makeshift stone shelters for the winter before moving down the loch to build the original *Caberfeidh* and *Cherrybank*.

Duncan was the brother of Sandy (below). In 1923, he married Christina (Teenie) MacKenzie, sister of the "Buie" brothers. Duncan crewed on the first *Thendara* as most of her crew were related through the "Buie" connections. Duncan's grandson Duncan has been recorded by the Ullapool Museum telling about his grandfather's trips on the *Thendara*. He mentions how the crew brought the yacht back to the Lochside for a short holiday after a summer season's racing.

Around 1924 Duncan and Teenie moved to Campbelltown on the other side of the loch to live in the cottages built by Pirie. Duncan stayed on the *Thendara* but worked for the Leckmelm estate during the winter. The family then moved to *The Sheiling* on Garve Road in Ullapool in 1936.

Left: Duncan "Bain" MacKenzie in Royal Navy uniform
(Ullapool Museum)

Right: Duncan "Bain" MacKenzie, later The Shieling, Garve Road, Ullapool
(Ullapool Museum)

Duncan and Teenie had three sons, William (Willie), Roderick (Roddy) and Colin. All married and brought up their families in Ullapool. Willie's children Duncan and Jackie, Roddy's children Derek and Elaine, and Colin's two boys Colin and David had yachtsmen on both sides of their father's family through the Buies and the Bains. Duncan died in 1978, followed by Teenie in 1993.

Sandy "Bain" MacKenzie (*Eileen*, others)

Alexander "Bain" MacKenzie (b. 1889) was the son of William and Johanna MacKenzie, and the brother of Duncan above. In 1942, when he was 53 and living at Ardindrean, he married 38-year-old Katy MacNab (daughter of Duncan and Johan) from Tor, Letters. They later moved to Pulteney Street, Ullapool. They had no children.

"Nelson" MacKenzies

Family Overview

John and Roderick MacKenzie were the sons of Letters crofter/fisherman John MacKenzie and his wife Catherine from Scoraig. This family lived at the croft next but one from *Southend* which now has the name *Tor Cottage*. There was another son Duncan who was killed in action in 1916 (aged 32) near the village of Buzancy in the area of the Somme.

Far left: Sandy
"Bain" MacKenzie,
Loggie,
later Pulteney
Street, Ullapool
(Ullapool Museum)

Left: Sandy "Bain"
MacKenzie
(Ullapool Museum)

Above: John "Nelson" MacKenzie
(Eric MacKenzie photo)

Left: Roderick "Nelson" MacKenzie in 1948
(Eric MacKenzie photo)

John "Nelson" MacKenzie (*Fedoa* and others)

John was the son of John and Catherine above. His brothers were Roderick and Duncan (killed in 1916), and he was therefore the uncle of Eric "Nelson" MacKenzie (b. 1932).

John served on an ammunition ship during World War One. On the yachts, John MacKenzie was at one time Skipper of *Fedoa* (built 1927) owned by Wordie and then MacLay. He lived at *The Anchorage*, Ardcharnich on Loch Broom.

Roderick "Nelson" MacKenzie (*Fiumara, Thendara, Molin* and others)

Roderick was the son of John and Catherine MacKenzie and was born at Letters. He was a cook and sailed on the cruising yachts (which generally raced only at the Clyde Fortnight), rather than the specialised racing yachts. Between the wars the yachts he crewed on included *Fiumara, Thendara, Roska* and *Fedoa*.

Roderick served in the Navy during World War One and was wounded during the Dardanelles/ Gallipoli campaign. His son Eric (below) also worked on the yachts after World War Two.

Above: Roderick MacKenzie in Torquay
(Eric MacKenzie photo)

Left: Roderick MacKenzie in RN uniform -
cap badge HMS VIVID – taken at Devonport
(Eric MacKenzie photo)

Above: Possibly onboard MAIMIE,
Roderick "Nelson" MacKenzie at right
(Eric MacKenzie photo)

Right: Large yacht (possibly OCEANA)
- crew group on foredeck Roddy
"Nelson" MacKenzie on right
(Eric MacKenzie photo)

Eric "Nelson" MacKenzie (*Ceol Mara, Fedoa*)

Eric (b. 1932) is the son of Roderick above. After World War Two he worked on the yachts for two years from age 15, starting on *Ceol Mara* in 1948. He also worked on the *Molin* and on the *Fedoa* where his uncle John was employed as Skipper.

Eric married Cathy MacLean and settled in Ladysmith Street, Ullapool. They had three children born in the 1960s; Roddy, Margaret and Rae, two of whom still live in Ullapool. Margaret has two daughters Ellie and Leah.

Eric MacKenzie – taken on
CEOL MARA after WW2
(Eric MacKenzie photo)

175

"Skene" MacKenzies

Kenny "Skene" MacKenzie (*Anna Marie, Roska*)

The "Sgean" or "Skene" MacKenzies were evicted from the fertile flat land of Newton at the Loch Broom Narrows in the 1800s.

Kenny "Skene" was born at 10 Loggie in 1900, son of Katie MacKenzie. He married Fanny Allan (b. 1907), and they spent their married life at Loggie. They had four children, Willie, Cathy, James and Alec. Several of Kenny's grandchildren continue to live in Ullapool; including Frances, Annette, Kenny, Ronnie and Audrey, along with great-grandchildren and great-great-grandchildren.

Kenny worked on the *Anna Marie* and *Roska* in the 1930s, and his son Alec sailed on the *Mariella* after the war.

Far left: Kenny
"Skene" MacKenzie
(Ullapool Museum)

Left: Kenny John
MacKenzie (Skene) in
ANNA MARIE jersey

Right: Kenny "Skene"
MacKenzie and Kenny
MacKenzie, both Loggie
(Ullapool Museum)

Other MacKenzies

John MacKenzie (*Uldra*)

John MacKenzie was the son of John Mackenzie of Loggie. He was born in 1870 and died young of TB in Glasgow in 1908.

His headstone in Clachan churchyard, Loch Broom identifies him as "*Captain of the Yacht ULDRA*" and bears the inscription "*erected as a token of esteem by James Robertson Blackie*".

Kenneth "Onorach" MacKenzie (*Rionnag na Mara*)

Coinneach an Onorach (Kenneth MacKenzie, 'the Honourable') was the Skipper of Alexander Pirie's yacht at one time.

In 1886, Coinneach an Onorach built up the house which is now called *Tigh Scoraig*, on Mill Street, Ullapool from a thatched cottage to its modern size. At that time it was named *Tighnabruaich*, possibly because of a yachting connection. He was the grandfather of Ullapool garage owner Jock MacKay whose descendants still live in the village.

Kenneth & John MacKenzie (*Sabine, Fedoa, Malista, Narcissus*)

Kenneth, the son of Roderick MacKenzie (Onorach) and Helen MacLean, was born at Leckmelm in 1851. Kenneth is listed as a yachtsman in the 1891 and 1901 census and is thought to have worked on the steam yacht *Sabine*. A painting of that vessel was found many years later in the family home. His two brothers Alexander and John were also yachtsmen, John being the father of John "Onorach" MacKenzie (Tor).

When Kenneth married Kenina Cameron in 1878, they moved to Ullapool and built *Seaside Cottage* on the Point where they brought up a family of nine. Their eldest son John (b. 1879) married Margaret Simpson and lived on the Point as well.

John worked for the Loch Tay Steamboat Company for several years until 1908. The summer seasons from 1926 until 1928 saw him working as Skipper on William Wordie's yacht *Fedoa,* followed by two years on the *Malista*. John also sailed on the big steam yacht *Narcissus*. Grandchildren of John still live in Ullapool; Catherine, Sandy and David "Lala" MacKenzie, and David's son Cameron as well as Nathan Chapple, a great-grandson.

John "Onorach" MacKenzie, Tor (*Thendara, Vida VI, Roska*)

John "Onorach" MacKenzie (1886 - 1959) lived at Tor, Letters. He was married to Robina MacKenzie (d. 1962), sister of the "Buie" MacKenzies who mostly crewed the *Thendara*. They had four sons, Iain, twins Roderick and Finlay, and Duncan.

References for John MacKenzie,
including from FEDOA Owner
(courtesy Sandy MacKenzie)

Above: John "Onorach" MacKenzie
with Robina & son Finlay - Note
EILEEN & ROSKA jerseys
(Ullapool Museum)

Left: John MacKenzie, 1912
(Ullapool Museum)

Sadly, John and Robina lost three sons during World War Two; Iain died aged 21 while serving in the Royal Air Force on the 8th November 1942, Roderick died at the Royal Naval Hospital in Gosport on 21st April 1943 aged 20 years, and Finlay was killed on 16th January 1945 aged 21 years while serving with the Royal Navy. Their surviving son Duncan "Tor" died with no issue.

John sailed on the *Thendara* and the *Vida*, and latterly the *Roska*. He would have been about 50 years old during the last pre-war years on the *Roska*.

This family was noted for their meticulous approach to everything. Their house and croft were kept extremely tidy. All the boys had an interest in the yachts, and being good at woodworking, they made models of them. One such model is in the Ullapool Museum collection.

"Onorach" is the Gaelic for "honest" or "honourable". The byname "Onorach" came down from his grandfather Roderick MacKenzie, who was married to Helen MacLean.

Right: Tidy Home of John
"Onorach" & Robina MacKenzie –
note steep lochside hills
(Ullapool Museum)

Below: Robina MacKenzie
with her four sons
(Ullapool Museum)

Edward MacKenzie (*Carraig*)

Edward Bayley Mackenzie (1892 - 1966) was from *Southend*, Letters. His father John (Iain) was a Skipper on the yachts, and at Edward's birth he is recorded as Master Yachtsman. His mother Catherine MacDonald was from Lochs, Lewis. Edward's older brothers Alick and Murdo were crewing at the yachts while Edward was still at school.

Edward MacKenzie
(Ullapool Museum)

During World War One the MacKenzie family were well represented in the different Forces. Alick served with the Lovat Scouts, and Murdo was on HM Transport ship *St Edmond*. Peter and William were in the Royal Navy, as was Edward, serving on mine-sweepers.

Kenneth joined the 4th Seaforth (Ross-Shire) Highlanders. John was killed in action at St Julien in October 1914, aged 28, while serving with the Highland Light Infantry.

After the war Edward worked on the yachts and continued to do so until after World War Two. He served as steward on shipbuilder James Lithgow's steam yacht *Carraig* for several decades, latterly working alongside Angie "Allan" MacKenzie.

During the 1930s and 1940s Edward had a motor launch at Letters, named *Nyanza II*. This boat may have been named after a P&O liner of the same name, built in 1907, or a yacht named *Nyanza* which was wrecked in the Pacific in 1890.

Ali Iain Mhor MacKenzie (*Thendara*)

Alick was a son of John (Iain in Gaelic) and a brother of Edward MacKenzie (above). He served in World War One with the Lovat Scouts. Alick was a piper, and used to walk up and down the road at Letters of an evening practising.

William "Black" MacKenzie (*Gleniffer, Valentine, Roska* and others)

William MacKenzie (1879 – 1953) was also known as Willie "Black". He was the son of John (d. 1910) and Margaret MacKenzie (d. 1895), Rhiroy. William married Bella MacKenzie in 1908, and they had children including William and Alexander (Lally). Bella died in 1974.

William crewed on cruising vessels (not the racing yachts) including the *Gleniffer* and latterly the *Roska*, on which he was Skipper. While employed on the *Gleniffer*, he painted an image of this impressive vessel under full sail. This painting remains in Ullapool.

In the 1930s William MacKenzie's own boat was named *Roska* (UL 69). This was a motor launch built at the Clyde yacht yard of Morris & Lorimer, Sandbank in 1925. She was 26ft keel

Left: Ali Iain Mhor MacKenzie (L) with Jackie "Buie" MacKenzie (R)

Right: Willie MacKenzie, skipper of ROSKA and father of Lally
(Ullapool Museum)

Below: Painting of GLENIFFER, made by William MacKenzie
(courtesy of Jessie Osborne & William Collier, GL Watson)

length, 6.9ft beam and 2.99 tons. The boat was fitted with a 12/14 Kelvin petrol-paraffin engine from new and was valued at £150 when registered in Ullapool in December 1931. William MacKenzie's address was then given as 4 Rhiroy. In March 1934 the registry was cancelled as she was no longer used for fishing.

Alec "Lally" MacKenzie (*Lulworth, Eileen, Ariana, Sheila, Vadura*)

Alexander John (Lally) MacKenzie was born in 1911, the son of William MacKenzie (above) and Bella MacKenzie, Rhiroy. Lally married Flora MacNab in 1942. She was the daughter of Duncan and Mary MacNab (nee MacRae) and a sister of Jimmy who died in World War Two. Lally lived on the Lochside at *Hazelbrae*, Ardindrean, and died in 2005 aged 94. Flora and Lally had one son; William James MacKenzie.

Lally crewed on several yachts including *Vadura, Ariana, Sheila* and *Lulworth*, and appears in many of the photographs in this book. He would have been about 19 when the *Lulworth* retired from racing in 1930.

Left: A young sailor Lally (Alec MacKenzie)
(Ullapool Museum)

Right: Lally (Alec MacKenzie) on rails of a yacht, possibly in south of England
(Ullapool Museum)

Willie "James" MacKenzie (*Thendara*)

Willie (James) MacKenzie was born in 1907 and lived at *Millburn Cottage*, Letters, the son of James MacKenzie and Annie MacLean. There was a big family of nine children. His father James had been crewing on yachts since the 1880s and three much older brothers; Simon, James and John, were all at the yachts in the early 1900s. There were also three brothers closer to Willie's age; Kenny, George and Murdo, who may also have continued in the family tradition of yachting work.

Willie James sailed on the *Thendara* in the 1930s. He later lived at *Hecla*, Pulteney Street, Ullapool. He was a painter/decorator and business partner of Roddy MacKenzie, West Shore Street.

Hugh (Huisdean) MacKenzie (*Ariana, Norseman, Roska*)

Hugh (1902- 1976) was the son of Hugh MacKenzie (son of John MacKenzie and Janet Ross) and Isabella MacKenzie (who was the daughter of Roderick "Buie" MacKenzie's brother Kenneth).

Huisdean lived at *Rowan Cottage*, Ardindrean, and sailed on the *Ariana, Norseman* and *Roska*. He married Isa Fraser from Torridon who he met when his yacht sailed into a loch in that area. Hugh was the father of Lochbroom locals Kate Rettie, Jock (the Hod) and Tommy MacKenzie, and grandfather to Fiona and Neil.

Hugh MacKenzie
(Ullapool Museum)

Hugh's uncle on the "Buie" side, William MacKenzie, also worked on the yachts as well as in the Merchant Navy. He served with the Royal Navy in the Great War. William died of malaria in 1915 and was buried at sea.

John "Jock" MacKenzie (*Vadura* and others)

John or Iain (1886 – 1974) was the son of Kenneth MacKenzie and Catherine MacNab. He was from Rhiroy and sailed on numerous yachts including *Vadura* and *Ceol Mara*. His brother William (Willie "Chisholm") was on the *Roska*. After the Second World War, John's son Willie (below) worked briefly on the yachts.

William "Jock" Mackenzie (*Kentra*)

Willie "Jock" MacKenzie, the son of John/Iain (above), went to the yachts after the Second World War and sailed on the *Kentra* in 1947. After doing one summer season on this yacht he went to the Merchant Navy, signing up with the Baron Line, owned by H Hogarth, who also owned the *Kentra*. Willie lives in Lochcarron.

John MacKenzie, Leckmelm (*Rionnag Na Mara*, others)

John MacKenzie was born in 1860 at Leckmelm, the son of Simon and Margaret MacKenzie. His grandfather Alexander, married to Catherine Ross, was a blacksmith and lotter at Leckmelm. John spent several years sailing deep sea, including trips to South America, and eventually became a Master Mariner. He was only 19 when A G Pirie purchased Leckmelm Estate in 1879, but he later worked on Pirie's steam yacht *Rionnag na Mara* (built 1886). As a Master Mariner he was well qualified to command a large vessel on long international voyages. At the time of his sudden death in 1920 from blood poisoning he was living at Mill Street, Ullapool and again working on the yachts.

John married Johanna MacLean in Coigach in 1885 and lived for a time on Isle Tanera but later moved to Shore Street, Ullapool. John and Johanna's daughter, Catherine MacLean married William MacKenzie whose parents came from the Lochside. William and his brother Alec were tailors in the then thriving Ullapool tailoring business. Catherine and William had four children including John and MacNab (Nabby, b. 1931). John and Nabby both had seafaring careers, and Nabby returned home to run excursion boats out of Ullapool for many years.

Descendants of John MacKenzie senior still live around Ullapool, including grandson Nabby and most of his children and grandchildren. John died in 2017 but is survived in the village by daughter Isabel and grandson Gregor.

John MacKenzie
with Landowner
and Yacht
Owner AG Pirie
(MacNab
MacKenzie photo)

Jimmy "Ferry" MacKenzie (*Thendara*)

James "Ferry" MacKenzie (1905-1984) was born at Rhireabhach in Scoraig. His father John MacKenzie (1858 - 1946) was known as "Fireman" on account of his job as a stoker in the engine room of the MacBrayne's steamers. He was originally from the Lochbroom Lochside (near Newton, Loggie), and had worked as a yachtsman like many from that area. John married Margaret MacKenzie (1864 - 1940) in 1886 and they lived at Loggie and Muncastle (Mungasdale) before moving to Scoraig in 1900, where they lived for about twenty years.

They had 12 children, 11 of whom survived into adulthood. Six sons and daughters emigrated to the USA, Peter was killed in the Great War, and Simon died of war wounds in 1932. The remaining family settled in Ullapool where they lived in the house named *Seabank* at 23 Shore Street, and ran the grocery shop next door until 1939. These buildings are located just west of the easternmost lane up to Argyle Street and are now the Youth Hostel.

Jimmy operated the Altnaharrie ferry to Ullapool for a time and was consequently known as "Jimmy Ferry". He served in the Royal Navy during World War Two and later became the Customs & Excise officer in Ullapool. He was an active member of the Lochbroom Sailing Club during the 1960s.

Jimmy married Catherine (Katie "Red") MacRae after she retired as Ward Sister at the Royal Northern Infirmary, Inverness. Jimmy died in 1984 and Katie in 2000. They had no children.

Jimmy "Ferry" MacKenzie (left)
(Ullapool Museum)

Kenneth John "Braes" MacKenzie (*Zara*)

Kenny was born in November 1903 to Donald MacKenzie and Flora MacDonald who were from Letters. Donald and Flora were living in Ullapool at the time but later moved to Campbeltown and then Lower Braes. Around 1907-1910, Donald was involved in the building of the extensive stone dykes on Beinn Dearg.

Kenny went away to work on the yachts and was on the steam yacht *Zara* for the 1927 and 1928 seasons. Sometime later he joined the Merchant Navy and travelled around the world on cargo ships for about ten years. Kenny's brother Murdo was also crewing on the yachts.

After he came ashore, Kenny became the ferryman for Isle Martin Flour Mill about 1937 and married Margaret MacKenzie from Gairloch in about 1938. By 1948 they had moved to Lower

Braes. They had three children Donald Fraser, Mary and Kenneth John (John Braes). Fraser, their oldest child (b. 1943), started his school life on Isle Martin.

Kenny has four generations of descendants living in Ullapool, including great-grandchildren Sean Stewart and Meghan MacCrimmon. Sean's two children are also descendants of Kenny MacKenzie (Skene).

MacLeans

Murdo "Clane" MacLean (*Vida VI*, others)

Murdo "Clane" was born in 1865 at Letters, the son of John MacLean and Mary MacRae. For over 20 years he crewed on the yachts, including the *Vida VI*. Murdo married Johan MacKenzie, Letters, who was a sister of Allan MacKenzie (Mor), and they lived at *Ault Dubh Cottage*, Ardindrean. He was therefore an uncle of Angie "Allan" MacKenzie. Three of their sons worked on the yachts; Johnny, Murdo and Simon. Murdo died in 1949, aged 84.

John "Clane" MacLean (*Vida VI*, *Roska*)

Johnny "Clane" was the son of Murdo (above) and Johan. He was born in Letters in 1913 and married Effie MacLennan who was the teacher at Ardindrean School. They lived on the Lochside, bringing up a family of three (Ally, Christine and John). Some of their descendants still live in Ullapool, including grandson Alan.

Johnny crewed on the *Vida VI* as well as working on the *Roska* for eight years, from soon after her build to the outbreak of war in 1939. He obtained his last letter of reference from the owner on Monday 18th September 1939, the same day as William MacGregor, and using the same language finding him to be, *"in every way satisfactory, willing and thoroughly honest"*.

Murdo "Tir Aluinn" MacLean (*Elfrida*, *Vida VI*, *The Ketch*)

Murdo MacLean was born in 1907, the brother of Johnny above. He was another Lochsider who went to the yachts but later joined the Merchant Navy.

In the summer season of 1925, when he was 17, Murdo crewed on the yacht *Elfrida*. The *Elfrida* was owned by William Raeburn, of Raeburn & Verel, who owned the Monarch Steamship Company. Raeburn also owned the steam yacht *Golden Eagle*. In November of that year, Murdo joined the Merchant Navy as an Able Seaman and did a fourteen month deep sea trip and three short coastal trips with the Monarch Line.

During the summer of 1928, Murdo crewed on William Wylie's sailing yacht *Vida VI* with Danie MacKenzie (Buie) as Skipper. Wylie was a very serious yachtsman and was known to take a thread from his silk scarf to judge the direction of the wind whilst sailing. The next fourteen

24, GEORGE SQUARE,
GLASGOW, C.2.

18th September, 1939.

TO WHOM IT MAY CONCERN

I have pleasure in stating that John MacLean has been with me as a yacht hand for eight years, latterly as cook steward.

I find him in every way satisfactory, willing and thoroughly honest, and I have no hesitation in recommending him for any job for which he may apply.

Upper: Murdo MacLean
in a ROSKA jersey
(Ullapool Museum)

Above, right: Reference letter
written for John MacLean
in September 1939
by Owner of ROSKA
(courtesy of his daughter
Christine Harvey)

Above, left: John MacLean
on ROSKA
(Ullapool Museum)

Right: John MacLean as
steward on ROSKA
(MacGregor photo)

RAEBURN & VÉREL, LTD.
STEAMSHIP OWNERS AND BROKERS
MONARCH STEAMSHIP CO., LTD.

WHR/DS

Telephones:
8671 Central (Trunk).
8672 Central (2 Lines).
Telegraphic Address:
"VERNAY, GLASGOW."

CODES:
Scott's 1906.   Watkins.
Standard Shipping.   A B C (5th Edition),
and Liebers.

45 WEST NILE STREET,

GLASGOW, c.1. 2nd October 1928

I have to certify that Murdo McLean served on board my yacht "ELFRIDA" for one season, 1925, as deck hand. I found him sober, attentive to his duties and in every way satisfactory.

William. H. Raeburn

Murdo MacLean references from William Raeburn for service on ELFRIDA, 1925 (courtesy Ian & Murdo MacLean)

Roddy MacLean (front right) on PANOPE (courtesy of Gordon Urquhart)

months saw Murdo again sailing deep-sea with the Merchant Navy, but during the summer season of 1930 he was back on the yachts, crewing on *The Ketch* with Peter Stewart as Master. One season Murdo crewed with Kenneth MacLeod (Raigie) from Letters.

When the Depression came, Murdo joined the Metropolitan River Police in 1930. While in London he married Lilian Rolles and eventually ran a café, but later returned north where he created the *Tir Aluinn* Hotel at Leckmelm. Murdo's son Ian, Ian's children Alasdair and Heather, and grandchildren still live around Ullapool.

Simon MacLean (*Vida VI*)

Simon (b. 1909) was a brother of Johnny and Murdo above. Like his brothers, he was a yachtsman and later worked for a yacht building firm in Southampton. Simon had no issue and retired back to Ullapool in the 1980s.

Roddy MacLean, Inverasdale (*Panope, Astra*)

Roddy MacLean (not related to the MacLeans above) was born in 1923 at Inverasdale to Kenneth (Kenny Gow) MacLean and Mary Ann Urquhart.

He moved to the south coast of England while working on the yachts. Roddy was a rigger (yacht mast builder and fitter) in Hamble, near Southampton and sailed on the big 23-Metre (later J-Class) boat *Astra* for a time. He continued to work on the yachts after the war, but in 1968 moved back to Scotland with his family. He lived at Ullapool, near his sister Rosie Urquhart, but sadly drowned while working on a fishing boat. Roddy had one daughter, Tessa.

Simon MacLean
(Ullapool Museum)

MacNabs

Families

Several MacNabs from Loggie and Letters worked on the yachts. The 1911 census has an Alick MacNab (sailor), aged 24, son of Duncan and Johan MacNab. This was probably Alexander MacNab who died in June 1973, aged 86.

Kenneth MacNab worked on the steam yacht *Zara* in 1914 with Kenneth MacRae and Willie "Black" MacKenzie.

Left: Kenneth MacNab, Letters
(Ullapool Museum)

Right: Ken MacNab (R) with (possibly) Hugh MacKenzie
(Ullapool Museum)

Duncan MacNab (*Pelagia, Roska, Venture*)

This Duncan MacNab (1901 - 1937) was the son of John MacNab and Maggie MacKenzie, and was born at Ardindrean. He had older brothers Alec and Ewen. Duncan was a cousin of Hugh "Huisdean" MacKenzie.

Duncan crewed on the *Venture* when she sailed around the north-west coast and Western Isles of Scotland in July 1931. He played the bagpipes and often entertained the owner and friends. A diary written by the owner mentions some yachts they encountered on that cruise: *Ben Hiant, Lochness, Vida, Medea, Roska* (MacGeorge family) and *Eileen* (Fulton family). It was recorded that the *Eileen* was a very "posh" boat. A copy of this diary can be found in the Ullapool Museum reference library.

Duncan also worked on the *Pelagia* and the *Roska*. He died of complications from an operation at Inverness Royal Northern Infirmary in February 1937. It is possible that his sudden death created the opening for William MacGregor of Scoraig to join the *Roska* in that year. Duncan was unmarried when he died.

Above: Duncan MacNab
on ROSKA
(Ullapool Museum)

Left: Duncan MacNab
(Ullapool Museum)

James (Jimmy) MacNab

Jimmy (1901 - 1940) was Alexander (Lally) MacKenzie's brother in law. His parents were Duncan MacNab (d. 1940) and Mary MacRae (d. 1959). They were married in 1897 and lived at Ardindrean. Two boys named Duncan died in 1900 and 1910, aged two and ten, respectively. There were also sisters Flora (who married Lally) and Annabella.

Jimmy crewed on the yachts, but he was lost at sea in World War Two when serving as 2nd Officer on SS *Moidart*. This coastal cargo steamer was sunk by a mine off East Anglia on the 27th July 1940 when on passage from Greenhithe to Newcastle with a cargo of cement. Including James, eleven men died, three of them from Skye.

Kenny "Skene" MacKenzie
& Jim MacNab
(Ullapool Museum)

Jimmy MacNab
(on left) with
others, including
Alec "Lally"
MacKenzie (4th
from left) & Alan
"Mor" MacKenzie
(back centre)
(Ullapool Museum)

Munros

John Munro (*Oceana*)

John Munro was the son of Simon Munro and Isabella Rose, and the nephew of Donald Rose (below). He was born in 1876 at Letters and went to the yachts as a young man, sailing on the *Oceana*. His brother Roderick who was born in 1888 also crewed on the yachts.

William Munro (*Hotspur*, *Morna* and others)

Willie (The Kaiser) Munro was born at Rhiroy in 1883, the son of John and Isabella Munro. His brother Alexander was the postman on the Lochside at one time. Willie's two sisters Jessie and Isabella married Danie and John MacKenzie, two of the "Buies". Willie had six children; Kenneth, Johnny, Jessie, Ella, Cathy and Betty.

He was a deck hand on the yachts all his working life and was employed on the *Hotspur* and *Morna* from Northern Ireland, as well as others.

Willie's son Kenneth had applied to join the Royal Air Force during World War Two but was not accepted. The reason was that when the children were younger they

John Munro on OCEANA
(Ullapool Museum)

William Munro from Rhiroy
in HOTSPUR RNIYC jersey
(courtesy Kenneth Munro)

contracted food poisoning from tinned corned beef and as a result Kenneth had to have his spleen removed. He worked for the Forestry Commission all his life. Kenneth married Lora and they had two sons Kenny and Martin in the 1960s. Kenny still lives in the Ullapool area and has three sons – Jamie, David and Michael.

Other Names

Campbells

Above: Hugh Campbell, Ardindrean, father of
Eric Campbell & Cathie Cameron, Hillview
(Ullapool Museum)

Left: Eric Campbell & crew of the IRIS –
possibly James Coats Junior's steam tug

Angus MacIntyre (*Rionnag Na Mara*)

Angus MacIntyre, Rhue (1848-1927) was one of the crew of Leckmelm laird Pirie's yacht *Rionnag na Mara* in the 1880s.

He was apparently at Vladivostok or some other exotic Russian port (more likely St Petersburg) when he had a chance encounter with another wandering seafarer from Wester Ross (Kenny 'Carpenter' MacKenzie originally of Ardessie, who came to Scoraig).

Angus MacIntyre MacLeod (1910-1999) of Ladysmith Street, Ullapool was a grandson of this Angus MacIntyre. The first of these MacIntyres rowed up from Mull to Ullapool in the 1790s (they belonged to the area around Loch Hourn).

John MacLeay (*Oceana*)

John MacLeay from Letters was born in 1860, son of Alexander MacLeay and Ann MacLennan. He was on the yachts for at least twenty years from 1891 or earlier. At one stage he was Skipper on the large vessel *Oceana*.

John married Christina Matheson, and three of their sons; Alec, Dan (Donald) and Kenneth, were all young men crewing on the yachts at the time of the 1911 census. The Great War intervened and Kenneth joined the Seaforth Highlanders, while Alec and Donald served on HM Transport ships.

Donald MacLeay

Donald MacLeay (1891 - 1917) grew up in Letters in the house now known as *"Lexie's"*. The last of the family to live there was Donald's sister Alexandra.

His father John MacLeay (above) was a yacht skipper, and the 1911 census shows John at Letters with his wife Christina and nine of their children. Donald (Dan) and his brothers Alick and Kenneth worked as yachtsmen each summer. Later, the three brothers served in World War One.

Donald MacLeay
(Records of the Men of Lochbroom)

Donald was in the Royal Navy, initially on the battlecruiser HMAS *Australia*. He was on HM transport ship *Thames* when she disappeared with all hands in August 1917. Donald was 26 years old and one of two young RNR men whose job was to operate the defensive gun that had been placed onboard. The *Thames* was on passage from Middlesbrough to France with a cargo of pig iron when she went missing. After the war, German Navy records revealed that the *Thames* had been sunk off the Humber Estuary by gunfire from the mine-laying submarine UC-63.

John MacLennan (*Thendara*, *Roska*, *Sheila*, others)

John "Poley" MacLennan (1886 - 1969) lived at *Ashcroft*, Letters. He was the son of Roderick MacLennan (d. 1926, aged 85) and Johan MacKenzie (d. 1939, aged 87) of Letters.

Before his family arrived, John had planned to move to Southampton to work permanently on the yachts. However, when his older brother Alex/Sandy (also a sailor) died in 1910, aged 26, he decided to stay at home to help his parents on the croft and take summer jobs on the Clyde yachts. John also had a sister Colina (died 1934, aged 57) and another brother Donald (died 1949, aged 68).

John sailed on the *Ariana, Roska* and *Sheila*, as well as some yachts from the Royal Burnham Yacht Club. Some trips included Spain, Sweden and the Norwegian fjords.

While working on the yacht *Dalga* in 1922, John married Annie MacKenzie in Glasgow. Annie was a sister of Allan "Mor" MacKenzie (she died in 1979, aged 89). They had a large family who had to be brought up on the £1 which John sent home each week. John's eldest son Alastair Iain drowned near Isle Martin in December 1970, aged 47. Greta (Margaret Murdina) was born in 1926 and went on to be a teacher. She married Duncan Stewart ("Dunkie Ara") in 1956 and had three children (Anne, Rory and Alan). Murdo married Rena MacGregor from Durnamuck in 1957. They lived at Letters on the Lochside, and had two children (Murdo, Kathleen).

Descendants of John's family still live at Letters and Ullapool, including daughter Greta, and grandchildren Rory Stewart, Tania Hutchison, Murdo MacLennan and Graham Hutchison.

Roderick (Rory Beag) and his sons were well known locally for building *Ashcroft* at Letters to exceptional quality in the early 20th century. The house is formed of red sandstone and contrasting blue-grey schist. Rory procured and shaped stone locally, but for particular sections he went further afield to a quarry near Altnaharrie. He cut and fashioned stone at this location for the lintels of the doors and windows. At low tide, the slabs were lashed to the outside of a boat pulled up on the beach next to the quarry. When the tide lifted, the boat was rowed or sailed back to the shore at Letters.

There was no road on the Lochside at that time; only a path along the shore and at the back of the houses. After landing the stone the lintels were carried up the steep slope of the croft to the house. It was physically

John MacLennan (left) with Lally (Alec MacKenzie) on steam yacht (Ullapool Museum)

very hard work and, as Rory was more than 60 years old at the time, his sons would have done most of the heavy lifting. Some thought that Sandy's early death in 1910 while the house was being built may have been due to overstrain from carrying these heavy weights.

James (Jimmy Cloudy) MacLeod (*Thendara*)

James MacLeod (1911 – 1998) was born at *Bayview*, Shore Street in Ullapool to Alexander and Isabella MacLeod. His father's occupation was recorded as "yachtsman".

Jimmy's grandparents, Catherine and Kenneth MacLeod (Kenneth Mor an Cuddichan), lived on Isle Martin until 1871 and then moved to Ullapool. Two of their daughters, Margaret and Ann, married two "Buie" MacKenzies from Letters. Margaret and Roderick MacKenzie (Buie) had ten children including skippers John/Jackie and Donald/Danie. Ann married Finlay MacKenzie, and so through both these marriages Catherine and Kenneth became the grandparents of many yachtsmen from the Lochside, which included MacLeods (Raigie), MacLeods (Ruagh) and MacKenzies (Buie).

Although Jimmy's father Alexander (Sandy Ruagh) was on the yachts, it was through his cousin Danie "Buie" MacKenzie that he began crewing. He volunteered to be mastheadsman because that paid a little extra money. Danie advised him to make the climb to the masthead for the first time at night so he could not see how precarious it was.

When he was in his mid-20s, Jimmy was mastheadsman on the *Thendara* when she won the Coronation Cup at Torbay in her debut year. This was an international regatta held to commemorate the crowning of King George VI in 1937. To mark the event a silver medal was struck, which today changes hands on the internet. The regatta attracted an entry list of 292 yachts including six 12-Metres, eight 6-Metres and fifteen yachts over 75 tons.

Jimmy's daughter Mary MacLeod recalled her father's story of the trophy race. It was a very still day with no wind, and all the yachts in the race were becalmed. One of the crew, from Lochinver possibly, or elsewhere in Sutherland (clearly some heathen Northern region), said he would call up a breeze, and he stabbed his knife into the mast and called on the witch Morven to give them wind. To the amazement of the men, the *Thendara* began to slip forward. Later, the crew (or at least the more enlightened Loch Broom men) decided that *Thendara* had twelve feet more height in the mast than the other yachts, and that their topsail had caught the first breath of wind. They won the race anyway.

In 1937 or 1938 the *Thendara* took a tour of the Baltic. While berthed in one of the German ports, possibly Travemunde or Swinemunde, they were near the German state yacht *Grille* when Hitler and his entourage came on board. Mary said her father watched them from the *Thendara's* masthead and later joked that if only he had had a rifle (he was an excellent shot), he could have prevented the Second World War.

Unfortunately, that war did come to pass, and along with many of his friends he served in the 51st Highland Division. During the Battle of France they fought on as the bulk of the British forces escaped at Dunkirk in late May and early June. With B Company of the 4th Seaforths, Jimmy took part in the assault on Abbeville on 4th June when he was seriously wounded. Only 17 out of 100 men in the Company were not killed or injured in this action, but Jimmy was fortunate to be rescued and treated. Due to his injuries he was discharged from service on his return to England.

He married Effie Campbell from Lewis, and they lived at Seaforth Road, Ullapool. Jimmy worked as a postman and died in 1998 aged 87. Effie died in December 2006, aged 92. They had two daughters; Mary and Donella, and four grandchildren.

Jimmy "Cloudy" MacLeod
(courtesy of Mary MacLeod)

Kenneth "Raigie" MacLeod

Kenny MacLeod was born on the Point, Ullapool in 1895 to Donald MacLeod and Alexandrina Munro. Kenny was a telegram boy in Ullapool when he was young and in 1914 went to the Great War with the 4th Seaforths. In 1931 he married Joanna MacIver from Coigach (daughter of Simon MacIver from Scoraig and teacher Mary Tullo) and settled in Ullapool.

Kenny was a joiner to trade but also crewed on the yachts. He worked with Murdo MacLean (*Tir Aluinn*) at one time, possibly on the *Vida*. One story tells of an occasion when they were on a yacht moored near Fort William. One evening the Owner's party rowed ashore and Kenny and Murdo decided to have a swim in their absence. As they had no swimming costume they improvised by pinning their vests down over their underwear. The Owners came back unexpectedly and so the Lochbroom men had to remain in the water hiding beside the boat until they had boarded and gone below.

Kenny "Raigie" MacLeod &
Joey MacIver, 1931

Kenny's son Donnie (former Harbour Master) died in 2019. His other son John still lives in Ullapool, as well as grandchildren Malcolm and Vivien, and great-grandchildren Danny, Alison and Connor. John has a grandson Taighan.

Kenneth MacRae (*Gleniffer, Zara*)

Kenneth MacRae (1862 – 1926) was the son of John MacRae and Ann MacDonald. He was from Letters and was an uncle of Allan "Mor" MacKenzie. His sister Margaret MacRae was the wife of Murdo "Allan" MacKenzie. Kenneth's brothers John and Duncan also worked on the yachts from the 1890s. They never married and stayed on the family croft at Letters.

Kenneth was sailing on the yacht *Oriana* in 1896. In later years he crewed on the Coats family's large schooner *Gleniffer* (built 1899). Kenneth's discharge book shows he sailed on the *Gleniffer* to the Baltic in both 1902 and 1903.

In the years 1902 - 1904 the Scottish Antarctic Expedition took place, led by William Spiers Bruce and funded by the Coats brothers. The *Gleniffer* welcomed the exploration ship *Scotia* back to Scotland in 1904. Kenneth again went abroad in 1914 on the Coats steam yacht *Zara*. Some of his fellow crewmen were Kenneth MacNab from Ardindrean and Willie MacKenzie (Black).

Kenneth married Mary MacDonald in 1897, and they had five children; one son Simon and four daughters. Mary died in 1911, aged only 44, and Kenneth died in 1926, aged 65.

Discharge Book of Kenneth MacRae – showing two voyages to Baltic on GLENIFFER (Ullapool Museum)

Donald Rose (*Katoomba*)

Donald Rose (1858 - 1949) was a fisherman and yachtsman, born on the Lochside. He was the son of Hugh Rose and Catherine MacDonald of Letters. Catherine died in 1861 and in 1865 Hugh (38) married Ann MacGregor (27) from Carnoch, Scoraig at Altnaharrie. Ann was the daughter of Duncan MacGregor and Janet MacDonald.

In 1883, Leckmelm landowner Pirie informed the Napier Commission how poor (in his opinion) seaweed was as a fertiliser, but in 1884 he took Hugh Rose to court for collecting seaweed from the shore of Pirie's estate. In February of that year the Lochside crofters were forbidden from collecting seaweed on the opposite shore at Leckmelm, as had been their habit for many years. A few months later they showed their defiance by sailing 15 boats to Leckmelm from Letters and Ardindrean, all flying flags and with a piper in the lead boat. The estate

Donald Rose (probably about 1903)
(Donald Miller photo)

workers were unable to prevent them from loading the boats with seaweed, and a policeman from Ullapool was sent for. The Lochside men were able to leave before the police arrived.

Before the road was built along the Lochside in the 1930s, Donald's boat was used to transport coffins along to Clachan Church for burial as it was the largest such boat in the area. Donald and his brother Duncan worked on the yachts, including the steam vessel *Katoomba* owned by the Clark family of Paisley. He later worked on the building of the railway to Kyle of Lochalsh (completed in 1897). It was there that he met his future wife, Margaret MacKay from Stromeferry (1881 – 1960).

Donald married Margaret in 1915, and they brought up their family in Letters. Their children were John, Katie Ann, Hugh and Donald. Son Donald (1922 - 2011) married Jessie MacKenzie in 1956 and worked as a forester around Loch Broom and then in the Inverness foundry. This Donald, together with Willie (James) MacKenzie, had a motor launch which they regularly sailed across to Ullapool on a Saturday for shopping, including paraffin oil for the Tilly lamps. There was no electricity on the Lochside in the 1940s.

Donald (Danny) Urquhart (*Panope, Merlin, Fiona, Fiumara*)

Danny, as he was known, was born at Glascarnoch in 1914 to Alexander Urquhart and Betsy Gillanders. Danny was a twin to Aulay but two months after their birth, their mother died. The twins were then separated, with Danny coming to live with his paternal grandmother Lexie Urquhart at Rhue, near Ullapool.

Left: Danny Urquhart (FIONA jersey) & Family
(Ann Urquhart)

Right: Danny Urquhart (back right) with MERLIN crew
(Ann Urquhart)

Danny crewed on several yachts as a cook, including the *Panope* and *Merlin*. The *Merlin* was a 104ft steam yacht owned in the 1930s by George Paisley, the Commodore of the Royal Western Yacht Club. Later Danny went to work on David MacBrayne's steamers and married and settled in Tobermory. He had a son Duncan. Dorrie, Ken and John Urquhart and Ernie Tolmie were his nephews. Danny has great nieces and nephews still living in Ullapool, including Ann Urquhart and Gordon Urquhart.

GLOSSARY

Aft or *After*
Backwards (stern or back part of the vessel)

Auxiliary
At the time, this was used to indicate the presence of an engine, more often to be found in a cruiser or cruiser racer. An auxiliary ketch would thus be primarily a sailing vessel with two masts and an auxiliary engine. The pure racing vessels had no engines.

Beam
Width of a boat.

Bermudan Rig
Sail rig, whereby the top of the mainsail comes to a point, giving the sail a triangular aspect, and set from the aft side of the mast. Began to displace gaff rig in yachting circles in the 1920s.

Big Class Yacht
In the first half of the 20th century, the large sailing yachts were given various names by the public – Big Boats, the Big Class, the Large Handicap Class, and so on.

Big Five
The Big Five label came from a famous photograph of the yachts *Lulworth, Britannia, Westward, White Heather II* and *Shamrock* taken by Beken of Cowes in 1926.

Boom
Horizontal spar at the foot of a sail. On a big yacht like the J-Class *Astra* this could be 30 inches deep and 6 inches wide.

Bowsprit
Spar extending forwards from bow.

Cheesecutter
A peaked cap worn by captains, mates and others in yachts etc. during the period covered by this book.

Clipper bow
A form of bow which rises from the water in a forward curving line (concave).

ON THE YACHTS

Composite
Method of construction using wood planks over metal frames, instead of all-wood or all-metal construction.

Counter
A form of stern used in sailing vessels.

Cutter
A type of single-masted sailing vessel (gaff or Bermudan rigged), with two sails forward of the mast.

Displacement
Weight of a boat and its contents (equal to the weight of water displaced).

Draught
The depth of the boat below the water line (depth of water required for the boat to float).

Fifes of Fairlie
A dynasty of Scottish yacht designers and builders based at Fairlie on the Ayrshire coast of the Firth of William Fife III, also known as Wm. Fife, Jr (1857 - 1944), was the third and last generation.

Fo'c'sle (Forecastle)
The forward compartment of a yacht's hull. In yachts of the era described this was the space where the professional crew usually lived.

Fore
Forward (bow or forwards part of the vessel).

Gaff rig
Sail rig, whereby the top of the sail is suspended from a yard, or gaff, which pivots around the main mast. The sail has a trapezoidal aspect. Began to be displaced by the Bermudan rig in the 1920s, but gaff rig designs continued to be built into the 1930s.

Gaff
The spar that supports the head of a gaff sail on the aft side of the mast. Hoisted and lowered up/down the mast by throat and peak halyards. On a big yacht this spar could weigh one tonne.

Halyard
Rope for hoisting sails.

Headsails
Sails at the fore end of the vessel – such as staysails, jib sails and jib topsails.

GLOSSARY

J-Class Yacht
A class of large yacht associated with the 1930s. The designs were based on a regulation called the American Universal Rule, which divided yachts into classes according to sail area, displacement, length and mast height. This resulted in an equivalent rating in feet, and the idea was that the yachts would be evenly matched for racing. Each class was notified by a letter of the alphabet. 'J' signified yachts with a waterline length of between 76 and 87 feet, LOA of 120 feet, displacement of up to 160 tons and an unrestricted sail plan. A total of ten J-Class yachts were built to compete for the America's Cup. Six of these were in the United States: *Enterprise, Weetamoe, Whirlwind* and *Yankee* in 1930, *Rainbow* in 1934 and *Ranger* in 1937. The four J-Class yachts built in the UK were *Shamrock V* in 1930, *Velsheda* in 1933, *Endeavour* in 1934 and *Endeavour II* in 1937. Some older big boats were altered to fit the J-Class, including *White Heather II, Britannia, Cambria, Candida* and *Astra*.

Jib Sail
A triangular sail set from the main mast head down the jib stay.

Jib Topsail
A triangular sail set from the topmast head down the fore topmast stay. Located above the jib sail. Racing yachts used to set three types of jib topsail – "long roper" (large), "baby" (small) and the "Yankee".

Keel
Lowest part of the boat. In a sailing yacht the keel is usually heavily ballasted with lead to enable the yacht to resist the overturning forces from the tall mast and sails.

Ketch
A type of two-masted sailing vessel (gaff or Bermudan rigged), with the shorter aft (mizzen) mast located forward of the rudder post.

Length over spars
Length of boat overall, including measuring out to tips of any spar (e.g. bowsprit) projecting over stern or bow.

Length overall (LOA)
Length of boat overall, excluding spars. Some owners and brokers (especially when selling) overstate this by using the dimension including the spars.

Length on deck (LOD)
Usually the same as the LOA. Less than the LOA if the Owner has overstated the LOA by including the spars.

Length Waterline (LWL)
Length of the boat at the waterline – usually less than LOA or LOD because of overhangs at bow and stern.

Luff
The forward edge of a sail.

Mastheadsman
A yacht sailor with special duties high in the rigging, leading to extra pay. Large yachts had a first and second mastheadsman.

Metre Class
A term signifying that the yacht design complied with the International Rule of 1907, which specified nine different boat classes (5, 6, 7, 8, 9, 10, 12, 15, 19 and 23 metre). The class bracket for each yacht was based upon a mathematical formula, incorporating length, beam, freeboard, and sail area. The resulting metre classification was broadly the same as the yacht's waterline length.

Mizzen
The after mast (in a two-masted vessel), or the sail set on the after mast.

Mylne, Alfred
Alfred Mylne (1872–1951) was a Scottish yacht designer, born in Glasgow. He was apprenticed to the Scottish shipbuilders Napier, Shanks and Bell, and went on to work as a draughtsman and apprentice to GL Watson, before setting up his own office in 1896. In 1906/7, Mylne was involved in establishing the International Metre Rule, a yacht-racing handicap rule. Mylne designed several race-winning boats, including the 19-Metre class cutter *Octavia* in 1911.

Port side
Left hand side of a boat when looking forwards.

Ratlines
Ropes secured horizontally on the shrouds supporting a mast to provide a "ladder" on which to climb the shrouds to the mast heads. Not usually provided in racing yachts.

Reef
To reduce the area of a sail by reefing. Reef points are provided at different heights above the bottom of the sail. The sail below the reef points is bunched up when reefed, thus reducing the sail area.

Schooner
A sailing vessel with two or more masts, with fore and aft sails (gaff or Bermudan rigged). The fore mast is shorter than the aft mast.

Sheet
The ropes which control the paying in or out of the sail relative to the centre of the boat. Mainsail is controlled by mainsheet, jib sail by jib sheets.

GLOSSARY

Shilling
A coin, with twenty shillings to the old pound. At decimalisation, the shilling was superseded by the decimal five-pence piece (twenty to the new pound) which had the same value.

Shrouds
The stays which support the mast in port and starboard directions. Before 1870 these were usually of natural fibre, and thereafter of steel.

Sixpence
Unit of currency. Half a shilling. Worth 2.5 new pence (post 1970s decimalisation). Since there were twenty shillings to the old pound and twelve pence to the shilling, there were 240 pence to the old pound. So, there were 40 sixpences to the old pound.

Spinnaker
Large, light balloon type foresail used when sailing downwind, especially in light airs. On a large yacht of the early 1900s, the boom for this sail could be 70 or 80 feet long and weigh one tonne. A racing skipper would want this assembly set and pulling in two minutes of his command.

Spreaders
A pair of horizontal struts supporting shrouds near the top of a mast.

Starboard side
Right hand side of a boat when looking forwards.

Staysail
Triangular sail secured on a stay between bow and masthead, forward of the foremast or mainmast.

Sloop
A type of single-masted sailing vessel (gaff or Bermudan rigged), with one sail forward of the mast.

Tacking
To turn a boat's bow through the wind so that the wind comes on the opposite side of the sails.

Thames Tonnage
A measure of the internal volume of a yacht – not its weight. Calculated from the main dimensions of the hull. Sometimes abbreviated to TM (Thames Measurement).

Tiller
Lever used to turn the rudder of a boat in order to steer it (used in the absence of wheel steering).

Topmast
In gaff rigged boats this was an additional mast set above the main element of the mast. Usually attached to fore side of lower mast and could be raised and lowered when required. Used to set gaff topsail (aft) and jib topsail (forward).

Topsail
A triangular sail set from the topmast above a gaff sail on the main or mizzen mast. This sail carried two spars to give it shape, and on a big racer the combined weight of this assembly could be one and a quarter tonnes.

Trysail
Very small sail made of strong canvas, used in stormy weather.

Yawl
A type of two-masted sailing vessel (gaff or Bermudan rigged), with the shorter after (mizzen) mast located aft of the rudder post.

REFERENCES

Books

1. *Alfred Mylne – The Leading Yacht Designers 1896-1920*, Ian Nicolson, Amberley, 2015

2. *Great Yacht Designs by Alfred Mylne 1921-1945*, Ian Nicolson, Amberley, 2016

3. *Lulworth - Classic Yachts*, François Chevalier, Thomas Reed Publications, ISBN 9 781408105 18 4, 2008

4. *Lulworth*, Andrew Rogers, Writewell Publications, ISBN 9 789090217 82 6, 2007

5. *Douglas Hume – A Personal History – The Howden Heritage*, David H Hume, printed by Nicholson & Bass, Belfast

    Contains short section detailing the post-war history of *Vadura* in Scotland

6. *Fast and Bonnie,* May Fife McCallum, John Donald, ISBN 085976 566 0, 1998

    History of the Fifes of Fairlie

7. *Stephen of Linthouse 1750-1950,* John L Carvel, privately published, 1951

8. *Stephen of Linthouse – A Shipbuilding Memoir,* Alexander Stephen, IESIS, Glasgow, ISBN 978 0 9932048-0-7, 2015

9. *The Salty Shore – The Story of the River Blackwater,* John Leather, Terence Dalton Ltd, ISBN 0 900963 52 2, 1979

    Contains valuable information about the Essex fishermen who crewed on (and also skippered) the big yachts, and the yachting scene

10. *The Auld Mug – The Scots and the America's Cup,* Len Patterson, Neil Wilson Publishing Limited, 2007

    Contains much information about the Scots challenges for the America's Cup, the Scots yacht designers and skippers, and life onboard the racing yachts

11. *Sailing Drifters,* Edgar J March, Percival Marshall, London, 1952

    Source of information about the designs, costs and income of the British herring fishing vessels at the end of the 19th century and early 20th century

12. *Shared Lives: Alexander Stephen, Shipbuilder & James Templeton, Carpet Maker,* Maureen Borland, Kilmarnock, ISBN 0 9552714 0 1, 2006

Articles and Papers

13. *Warshipbuilding on the Clyde 1889-1939 – A Financial Study,* Hugh Peebles, 31st January 1986

    Research paper analysing archived shipyard accounts, including results of Stephen, Linthouse for *Vadura, Fiumara,* and *Thendara*

14. *Mariquita and The Big Four,* John Leather, *Classic Boat,* April 2008

    Development of 19-Metre class and relation to 15-Metre and 23-Metre classes, with crew sizes, races and costs

15. *Robertson's Boat Yard 1876-1980*, by David Hutchinson, *Classic Boat*, June 2008
16. *The English Yachting Narrative with Particular Reference to Cornwall*, Michael Bender, published in *Troze*, the journal of the National Maritime Museum Cornwall, Volume 1, No. 4, June 2009
17. *All Aboard, 25 Beautiful Homes* magazine, IPC Media, October 1998
    Article on *Hotspur* as houseboat
18. *Magnificent Yachts of the West*, Iain Thornber, *Oban Times*, 2nd November 2017
    Article on the yachts with connections to the Oban and Ardnamurchan areas
19. *Ullapool, Loch Broom*, James Mathieson, published by *Ullapool News*, 1975
    Short history of Ullapool area

WEBSITES

http://ullapoolmuseum.co.uk/our-collection/
Ullapool Museum searchable collection of photographs contributed by locals, including many of yachting work and yachting families

www.Ambaile.org.uk
Contains some yachting related photographs from Ullapool Museum Photographic Collection

www.classicyachtinfo.com
Pictures and history of many old yachts

www.clydeships.co.uk
Details of ships and yachts built in Scotland

http://www.sythendara.com
Several interesting old photos of Thendara with crew and guests

http://www.dalmadan.com/?p=4755
Clyde river maritime history – section on yachting

www.Lulworth.nl
Website containing much information and photographs regarding the history and restoration of Lulworth

http://www.aniodhlann.org.uk/tag/oceana/
Tiree website – section on loss of Oceana

https://www.fky.org/freundeskreis/nachgefragt-fortuna.htm
History of Tritonia (also named Jeano), David Hutchinson, Updated 26 Aug 2009

Robertson's Yard Boat Database, currently under development
Contact robyardsb@hotmail.co.uk for further details or with contributions.

INDEX